Preparing for Easter

ALSO BY C. S. LEWIS

Compelling Reason
Christian Reflections
The Four Loves
The Great Divorce
Miracles
The Pilgrim's Regress
The Problem of Pain
The Screwtape Letters
Screwtape Proposes a Toast
Surprised by Joy
The Weight of Glory

The Chronicles of Narnia:
The Lion, the Witch and the Wardrobe
Prince Caspian
The Voyage of the Dawn Treader
The Silver Chair
The Horse and His Boy
The Magician's Nephew
The Last Battle

The Cosmic Trilogy:
Out of the Silent Planet
Perelandra
That Hideous Strength

Preparing for Easter

FIFTY DEVOTIONAL READINGS FROM C. S. LEWIS

C. S. Lewis

WILLIAM COLLINS

William Collins
An imprint of HarperCollins*Publishers*
1 London Bridge Street
London SE1 9GF

WilliamCollinsBooks.com

First published in the United States of America by HarperOne, an imprint of
HarperCollins*Publishers*, in 2017

First published in Great Britain by William Collins in 2017

1

A catalogue record of this book is available from the British Library

ISBN 978-0-00-826321-8

Designed by Yvonne Chan

Printed and bound by CPI Group (UK) Ltd, Croydon, CR0 4YY

MIX
Paper from
responsible sources
FSC C007454

Contents

Preface

People often describe C. S. Lewis as the greatest Christian apologist of the twentieth century. And he clearly deserves such a title, since Lewis provided the groundwork for many thoughtful Christians for why the Christian faith not only remains intellectually credible but also provides the best vantage point for seeing and understanding our world today. This is certainly one of the main reasons for explaining the very strange phenomenon of an author selling many more copies of such works as *Mere Christianity*, *The Screwtape Letters*, *The Great Divorce*, and *The Four Loves* today than during the author's own lifetime. Since HarperCollins, Lewis's publisher in both the United States and the United Kingdom, is celebrating its two-hundredth anniversary in 2017, we can say very confidently that Lewis's growing and continued popularity is very rare indeed.

But being a leading Christian defender of the faith would not be the only reason to explain Lewis's posthumous popularity. Like Lewis's contemporary, Dietrich Bonhoeffer, Lewis was also a pioneering explainer of the Christian life itself. In fact, I believe that Lewis's apologetics are so powerful precisely because many find his vision of the Christian life so compelling and inspiring.

It is this latter role of Lewis's, as a visionary prophet for how to follow Christ today, that this collection is concerned with. In many Christian traditions, the period before Easter is seen as a time of spiritual preparation for the day we later celebrate and welcome the "grand miracle" Christ accomplished through the cross. In these anticipatory days, often called Lent, many Christians choose the spiritual discipline of reading a devotional work each morning to help keep their focus on God. In *Preparing for Easter*, we have put together fifty readings from a broad swath of Lewis's works, many of which come from books and essays that few people encounter but which still embody Lewis's characteristic wisdom, for just this purpose.

The selections come to us from the skilled editorial eye of Zachry Kincaid, the Lewis expert who edits the popular blog on our website CSLewis.com. We hope you enjoy these selections and that they help you, as Lewis would say, go "further up and further in" to the world God invites us to enter.

MICHAEL G. MAUDLIN
Senior Vice President and Executive Editor
HarperOne, an Imprint of HarperCollins Publishers

WEEK ONE

Getting Closer to God

Scripture Readings
Matthew 11:27–30
Psalm 90:1–6

Every Christian would agree that a man's spiritual health is exactly proportional to his love for God. But man's love for God, from the very nature of the case, must always be very largely, and must often be entirely, a Need-love. This is obvious when we implore forgiveness for our sins or support in our tribulations. But in the long run it is perhaps even more apparent in our growing—for it ought to be growing—awareness that our whole being by its very nature is one vast need; incomplete, preparatory, empty yet cluttered, crying out for Him who can untie things that are now knotted together and tie up things that are still dangling loose. I do not say that man can never bring to God anything at all but sheer Need-love. Exalted souls may tell us of a reach beyond that. But they would also, I think, be the first to tell us that those heights would cease to be true Graces, would become Neo-Platonic or finally diabolical illusions, the moment a man dared to think that he could live on them and henceforth drop out the element of need. 'The highest,' says the Imitation, 'does not stand without the lowest.' It would be a bold and silly creature that came before its Creator with the boast 'I'm no beggar. I love you disinterestedly.' Those who come nearest to a Gift-love for God will next moment, even at the very same moment, be beating their breasts with the publican and laying their indigence before the only real Giver. And God will have it so. He addresses our Need-love: 'Come unto me all ye that travail and are heavy-laden,' or, in the Old Testament, 'Open your mouth wide and I will fill it.' Thus one Need-love, the greatest of all, either coincides with or at least makes a main ingredient in man's highest, healthiest, and most realistic spiritual condition. A very strange corollary follows. Man approaches God most nearly when he is in one sense least like God. For what can be more unlike than fullness and need, sovereignty and humility, righteousness and penitence, limitless power and a cry for help? This paradox staggered me when I first ran into it; it also wrecked all my previous attempts to write about love. When we face it, something like this seems to result.

We must distinguish two things which might both possibly be called 'nearness to God'. One is likeness to

4

God. God has impressed some sort of likeness to Himself, I suppose, in all that He has made. Space and time, in their own fashion, mirror His greatness; all life, His fecundity; animal life, His activity. Man has a more important likeness than these by being rational. Angels, we believe, have likenesses which Man lacks: immortality and intuitive knowledge. In that way all men, whether good or bad, all angels including those that fell, are more like God than the animals are. Their natures are in this sense 'nearer' to the Divine Nature. But, secondly, there is what we may call nearness of approach. If this is what we mean, the states in which a man is 'nearest' to God are those in which he is most surely and swiftly approaching his final union with God, vision of God, and enjoyment of God. And as soon as we distinguish nearness-by-likeness and nearness-of-approach, we see that they do not necessarily coincide. They may or may not.

Perhaps an analogy may help. Let us suppose that we are doing a mountain walk to the village which is our home. At mid-day we come to the top of a cliff where we are, in space, very near it because it is just below us. We could drop a stone into it. But as we are no cragsmen we can't get down. We must go a long way round; five miles, maybe. At many points during that *détour* we shall, statically, be far further from the village than we were when we sat above the cliff. But only statically.

In terms of progress we shall be far 'nearer' our baths and teas.

Since God is blessed, omnipotent, sovereign, and creative, there is obviously a sense in which happiness, strength, freedom, and fertility (whether of mind or body), wherever they appear in human life, constitute likenesses, and in that way proximities, to God. But no one supposes that the possession of these gifts has any necessary connection with our sanctification. No kind of riches is a passport to the Kingdom of Heaven.

At the cliff's top we are near the village, but however long we sit there we shall never be any nearer to our bath and our tea. So here the likeness, and in that sense nearness, to Himself which God has conferred upon certain creatures and certain states of those creatures is something finished, built in. What is near Him by likeness is never, by that fact alone, going to be any nearer. But nearness of approach is, by definition, increasing nearness. And whereas the likeness is given to us—and can be received with or without thanks, can be used or abused—the approach, however initiated and supported by Grace, is something we must do. Creatures are made in their varying ways images of God without their own collaboration or even consent. It is not so that they become sons of God. And the likeness they receive by sonship is not that of images or portraits. It is in one way more than likeness, for it is unison or unity with God in will; but this is consistent with all the differences we have been considering. Hence, as a better writer has said, our imitation of God in this life—that is, our willed imitation as distinct from any of the likenesses which He has impressed upon our natures or states—must be an imitation of God incarnate: our model is the Jesus, not only of Calvary, but of the workshop, the roads, the crowds, the clamorous demands and surly oppositions, the lack of all peace and privacy, the interruptions. For this, so strangely unlike anything we can attribute to the Divine life in itself, is apparently not only like, but is, the Divine life operating under human conditions.

THE FOUR LOVES
"Introduction"

Embracing Glory

Scripture Readings
Romans 8:22–27
Psalms 1:1–3

In the first place, we ask how the Nature created by a good God comes to be in this condition? By which question we may mean either how she comes to be imperfect—to leave 'room for improvement' as the schoolmasters say in their reports—or else, how she comes to be positively depraved. If we ask the question in the first sense, the Christian answer (I think) is that God, from the first, created her such as to reach her perfection by a process in time. He made an Earth at first 'without form and void' and brought it by degrees to its perfection. In this, as elsewhere, we see the familiar pattern—descent from God to the formless Earth and reascent from the formless to the finished. In that sense a certain degree of 'evolutionism' or 'developmentalism' is inherent in Christianity. So much for Nature's imperfection; her positive depravity calls for a very different explanation. According to the Christians this is all due to sin: the sin both of men and of powerful, non-human beings, supernatural but created. The unpopularity of this doctrine arises from the widespread Naturalism of our age—the belief that nothing but Nature exists and that if anything else did she is protected from it by a Maginot Line—and will disappear as this error is corrected. To be sure, the morbid inquisitiveness about such beings which led our ancestors to a pseudo-science of Demonology, is to be sternly discouraged: our attitude should be that of the sensible citizen in wartime who believes that there are enemy spies in our midst but disbelieves nearly every particular spy story. We must limit ourselves to the general statement that beings in a different, and higher 'Nature' which is *partially* interlocked with ours have, like men, fallen and have tampered with things inside our frontier. The doctrine, besides proving itself fruitful of good in each man's spiritual life, helps to protect us from shallowly optimistic or pessimistic views of Nature. To call her either 'good' or 'evil' is boys' philosophy. We find ourselves in a world of transporting pleasures, ravishing beauties, and tantalising possibilities, but all constantly being destroyed, all coming to nothing. Nature has all the air of a good thing spoiled.

The sin, both of men and of angels, was rendered possible by the fact that God gave them free will: thus surrendering a portion of His omnipotence (it is again a death-like or descending movement) because He saw that from a world of free creatures, even though they fell, He could work out (and this is the reascent) a deeper happiness and a fuller splendour than any world of automata would admit.

Another question that arises is this. If the redemption of Man is the beginning of Nature's redemption as a whole, must we then conclude after all that Man is the most important thing in Nature? If I had to answer 'Yes' to this question I should not be embarrassed. Supposing Man to be the only rational animal in the universe, then (as has been shown) his small size and the small size of the globe he inhabits would not make it ridiculous to regard him as the hero of the cosmic drama: Jack after all is the smallest character in *Jack the Giant-Killer*. Nor do I think it in the least improbable that Man is in fact the only rational creature in this spatio-temporal Nature. That is just the sort of lonely pre-eminence—just the disproportion between picture and frame—which all that I know of Nature's 'selectiveness' would lead me to anticipate.

But I do not need to assume that it actually exists. Let Man be only one among a myriad of rational species, and let him be the only one that has fallen. Because he has fallen, for him God does the great deed; just as in the parable it is the one lost sheep for whom the shepherd hunts. Let Man's pre-eminence or solitude be one not of superiority but of misery and evil: then, all the more, Man will be the very species into which Mercy will descend. For this prodigal the fatted calf, or, to speak more suitably, the eternal Lamb, is killed. But once the Son of God, drawn hither not by our merits but by our unworthiness, has put on human nature, then our species (whatever it may have been before) does become in one sense the central fact in all Nature: our species, rising after its long descent, will drag all Nature up with it because in our species the Lord of Nature is now included. And it would be all of a piece with what we already know if ninety and nine righteous races inhabiting distant planets that circle distant suns, and needing no redemption on their own account, were remade and glorified by the glory which had descended into our race. For God is not merely mending, not simply restoring a *status quo*. Redeemed humanity is to be something more glorious than unfallen humanity would have been, more glorious than any unfallen race now is (if at this moment the night sky conceals any such). The greater the sin, the greater the mercy: the deeper the death, the brighter the rebirth. And this super-added glory will, with true vicariousness, exalt all creatures and those who have never fallen will thus bless Adam's fall.

MIRACLES
"The Grand Miracle"

FRIDAY

On Perfection

Scripture Readings
Matthew 5:43–48
Psalm 19:1–8

When I was a child I often had toothache, and I knew that if I went to my mother she would give me something which would deaden the pain for that night and let me get to sleep. But I did not go to my mother—at least, not till the pain became very bad. And the reason I did not go was this. I did not doubt she would give me the aspirin; but I knew she would also do something else. I knew she would take me to the dentist next morning. I could not get what I wanted out of her without getting something more, which I did not want. I wanted immediate relief from pain: but I could not get it without having my teeth set permanently right. And I knew those dentists: I knew they started fiddling about with all sorts of other teeth which had not yet begun to ache. They would not let sleeping dogs lie, if you gave them an inch they took an ell.

12

Now, if I may put it that way, Our Lord is like the dentists. If you give Him an inch, He will take an ell. Dozens of people go to Him to be cured of some one particular sin which they are ashamed of (like masturbation or physical cowardice) or which is obviously spoiling daily life (like bad temper or drunkenness). Well, He will cure it all right: but He will not stop there. That may be all you asked; but if once you call Him in, He will give you the full treatment.

That is why He warned people to 'count the cost' before becoming Christians. 'Make no mistake,' He says, 'if you let me, I will make you perfect. The moment you put yourself in My hands, that is what you are in for. Nothing less, or other, than that. You have free will, and if you choose, you can push Me away. But if you do not push Me away, understand that I am going to see this job through. Whatever suffering it may cost you in your earthly life, whatever inconceivable purification it may cost you after death, whatever it costs Me, I will never rest, nor let you rest, until you are literally perfect—until my Father can say without reservation that He is well pleased with you, as He said He was well pleased with me. This I can do and will do. But I will not do anything less.'

And yet—this is the other and equally important side of it—this Helper who will, in the long run, be satisfied with nothing less than absolute perfection, will also be delighted with the first feeble, stumbling effort you make tomorrow to do the simplest duty. As a great Christian writer (George MacDonald) pointed out, every father is pleased at the baby's first attempt to walk: no father would be satisfied with anything less than a firm, free, manly walk in a grown-up son. In the same way, he said, 'God is easy to please, but hard to satisfy.'

The practical upshot is this. On the one hand, God's demand for perfection need not discourage you in the least in your present attempts to be good, or even in your present failures. Each time you fall He will pick you up again. And He knows perfectly well that your own efforts are never going to bring you anywhere near perfection. On the other hand, you must realise from the outset that the goal towards which He is beginning to guide you is absolute perfection; and no power in the whole universe, except you yourself, can prevent Him from taking you to that goal. That is what you are in for. And it is very important to realise that. If we do not, then we are very likely to start pulling back and resisting Him after a certain point. I think that many of us, when Christ has enabled us to overcome one or two sins that were an obvious nuisance, are inclined to feel (though we do not put it into words) that we are now good enough. He has done all we wanted Him to do, and we should be obliged if He would now leave us alone. As we say, 'I never expected to be a saint, I only wanted to be a decent ordinary chap.' And we imagine when we say this that we are being humble.

But this is the fatal mistake. Of course we never wanted, and never asked, to be made into the sort of creatures He is going to make us into. But the question is not what we intended ourselves to be, but what He intended us to be when He made us. He is the inventor, we are only the machine. He is the painter, we are only the picture. How should we know what He means us to be like? You see, He has already made us something very different from what we were. Long ago, before we were born, when we were inside our mothers' bodies, we passed through various stages. We were once rather like vegetables, and once rather like fish: it was only at a later stage that we became like human babies. And if we had been conscious at those earlier stages, I daresay we should have been quite contented to stay as vegetables or fish—should not have wanted to be made into babies. But all the time He knew His plan for us and was determined to carry it out. Something the same is now happening at a higher level. We may be content to remain what we call 'ordinary people': but He is determined to carry out a quite different plan. To shrink back from that plan is not humility: it is laziness and cowardice. To submit to it is not conceit or megalomania; it is obedience.

MERE CHRISTIANITY
"Counting the Cost"

Rejoicing in Judgement

 Scripture Readings
Matthew 25:31–46
Psalm 67:1–7

If there is any thought at which a Christian trembles it is the thought of God's 'judgement'. The 'Day' of Judgement is 'that day of wrath, that dreadful day'. We pray for God to deliver us 'in the hour of death and at the day of judgement'. Christian art and literature for centuries have depicted its terrors. This note in Christianity certainly goes back to the teaching of Our Lord Himself; especially to the terrible parable of the Sheep and the Goats. This can leave no conscience untouched, for in it the 'Goats' are condemned entirely for their sins of omission; as if to make us fairly sure that the heaviest charge against each of us turns not upon the things he has done but on those he never did—perhaps never dreamed of doing.

It was therefore with great surprise that I first noticed how the Psalmists talk about the judgements of God.

They talk like this; 'O let the nations rejoice and be glad, for thou shalt judge the folk righteously' (Ps. 67:4), 'Let the field be joyful . . . all the trees of the wood shall rejoice before the Lord, for he cometh, for he cometh to judge the earth' (Ps. 96:12, 13). Judgement is apparently an occasion of universal rejoicing. People ask for it: 'Judge me, O Lord my God, according to thy righteousness' (Ps. 35:24).

The reason for this soon becomes very plain. The ancient Jews, like ourselves, think of God's judgement in terms of an earthly court of justice. The difference is that the Christian pictures the case to be tried as a criminal case with himself in the dock; the Jew pictures it as a civil case with himself as the plaintiff. The one hopes for acquittal, or rather for pardon; the other hopes for a resounding triumph with heavy damages. Hence he prays 'judge my quarrel', or 'avenge my cause' (Ps. 35:23). And though, as I said a minute ago, Our Lord in the parable of the Sheep and the Goats painted the characteristically Christian picture, in another place He is very characteristically Jewish. Notice what He means by 'an unjust judge'. By those words most of us would mean someone like Judge Jeffreys or the creatures who sat on the benches of German tribunals during the Nazi régime: someone who bullies witnesses and jurymen in order to convict, and then savagely to punish, innocent men. Once again, we are thinking of a criminal trial. We hope we shall never appear in the dock before such a judge. But the Unjust Judge in the parable is quite a different character. There is no danger of appearing in his court against your will: the difficulty is the opposite—to get into it. It is clearly a civil action. The poor woman (Luke 18:1–5) has had her little strip of land—room for a pigsty or a hen-run—taken away from her by a richer and more powerful neighbour (nowadays it would be Town-Planners or some other 'Body'). And she knows she has a perfectly watertight case. If once she could get it into court and have it tried by the laws of the land, she would be bound to get that strip back. But no one will listen to her, she can't get it tried. No wonder she is anxious for 'judgement'.

Behind this lies an age-old and almost world-wide experience which we have been spared. In most places and times it has been very difficult for the 'small man' to get his case heard. The judge (and, doubtless, one or two of his underlings) has to be bribed. If you can't afford to 'oil his palm' your case will never reach court. Our judges do not receive bribes. (We probably take this blessing too much for granted; it will not remain with us automatically.) We need not therefore be surprised if the Psalms, and the Prophets, are full of the longing for judgement, and regard the announcement that 'judgement' is coming as good news. Hundreds and thousands of people who have been stripped of all they possess and who have the right entirely on their side will at last be heard. Of course they are not afraid of judgement. They know their case is unanswerable—if only it could be heard. When God comes to judge, at last it will.

Dozens of passages make the point clear. In Psalm 9 we are told that God will 'minister true judgement' (8), and that is because He 'forgetteth not the complaint of the poor' (12). He 'defendeth the cause' (that is, the 'case') 'of the widows' (Ps. 68:5). The good king in Psalm 72:2 will 'judge' the people rightly; that is, he will 'defend the poor'. When God 'arises to judgement' he will 'help all the meek upon earth' (Ps. 76:9), all the timid, helpless people whose wrongs have never been righted yet. When God accuses earthly judges of 'wrong judgement', He follows it up by telling them to see that the poor 'have right' (Ps. 82:2, 3).

The 'just' judge, then, is primarily he who rights a wrong in a civil case. He would, no doubt, also try a criminal case justly, but that is hardly ever what the Psalmists are thinking of. Christians cry to God for mercy instead of justice; *they* cried to God for justice instead of injustice. The Divine Judge is the defender, the rescuer. Scholars tell me that in the Book of Judges the word we so translate might almost be rendered 'champions'; for though these 'judges' do sometimes perform what we should call judicial functions, many of them are much more concerned with rescuing the oppressed Israelites from Philistines and others by force of arms. They are more like Jack the Giant Killer than like a modern judge in a wig. The knights in romances of chivalry who go about rescuing distressed damsels and widows from giants and other tyrants are acting almost as 'judges' in the old Hebrew sense: so is the modern solicitor (and I have known such) who does unpaid work for poor clients to save them from wrong.

I think there are very good reasons for regarding the Christian picture of God's judgement as far more profound and far safer for our souls than the Jewish. But this does not mean that the Jewish conception must simply be thrown away. I, at least, believe I can still get a good deal of nourishment out of it.

It supplements the Christian picture in one important way. For what alarms us in the Christian picture is the infinite purity of the standard against which our actions will be judged. But then we know that none of us will ever come up to that standard. We are all in the same boat. We must all pin our hopes on the mercy of God and the work of Christ, not on our own goodness. Now the Jewish picture of a civil action sharply reminds us that perhaps we are faulty not only by the Divine standard (that is a matter of course) but also by a very human standard which all reasonable people admit and which we ourselves usually wish to enforce upon others. Almost certainly there are unsatisfied claims, human claims, against each one of us. For who can really believe that in all his dealings with employers and employees, with husband or wife, with parents and children, in quarrels and in collaborations, he has always attained (let alone charity or generosity) mere honesty and fairness? Of course we forget most of the injuries we have done. But the injured parties do not forget even if they forgive. And God does not forget. And even what we can remember is formidable enough. Few of us have always, in full measure, given our pupils or patients or clients (or whatever our particular 'consumers' may be called) what we were being paid for. We have not always done quite our fair share of some tiresome work if we found a colleague or partner who could be beguiled into carrying the heavy end.

Our quarrels provide a very good example of the way in which the Christian and Jewish conceptions differ, while yet both should be kept in mind. As Christians we must of course repent of all the anger, malice, and self-will which allowed the discussion to become, on our side, a quarrel at all. But there is also the question on a far lower level: 'granted the quarrel (we'll go into that later) did you fight fair?' Or did we not quite unknowingly falsify the whole issue? Did we pretend to be angry about one thing when we knew, or could have known, that our anger had a different and much less presentable cause? Did we pretend to be 'hurt' in our sensitive and tender feelings (fine natures like ours are so vulnerable) when envy, ungratified vanity, or thwarted self-will was our real trouble? Such tactics often succeed. The other parties give in. They give in not because they don't know what is really wrong with us but because they have long known it only too well, and that sleeping dog can be roused, that skeleton brought out of its cupboard, only at the cost of imperilling their whole relationship with us. It needs surgery which they know we will never face. And so we win; by cheating. But the unfairness is very deeply felt. Indeed what is commonly called 'sensitiveness' is the most powerful engine of domestic tyranny, sometimes a lifelong tyranny. How we should deal with it in others I am not sure; but we should be merciless to its first appearances in ourselves.

REFLECTIONS ON THE PSALMS
"'Judgement' in the Psalms"

WEEK TWO

Becoming a Follower of God

Scripture Readings
Philippians 2:1–11
Psalm 18:6–11

The Son of God became a man to enable men to become sons of God. We do not know—anyway, I do not know—how things would have worked if the human race had never rebelled against God and joined the enemy. Perhaps every man would have been 'in Christ', would have shared the life of the Son of God, from the moment he was born. Perhaps the Bios or natural life would have been drawn up into the Zoe, the uncreated life, at once and as a matter of course. But that is guesswork. You and I are concerned with the way things work now.

And the present state of things is this. The two kinds of life are now not only different (they would always have been that) but actually opposed. The natural life in each of us is something self-centred, something that

25

wants to be petted and admired, to take advantage of other lives, to exploit the whole universe. And especially it wants to be left to itself: to keep well away from anything better or stronger or higher than it, anything that might make it feel small. It is afraid of the light and air of the spiritual world, just as people who have been brought up to be dirty are afraid of a bath. And in a sense it is quite right. It knows that if the spiritual life gets hold of it, all its self-centredness and self-will are going to be killed and it is ready to fight tooth and nail to avoid that.

Did you ever think, when you were a child, what fun it would be if your toys could come to life? Well suppose you could really have brought them to life. Imagine turning a tin soldier into a real little man. It would involve turning the tin into flesh. And suppose the tin soldier did not like it. He is not interested in flesh: all he sees is that the tin is being spoilt. He thinks you are killing him. He will do everything he can to prevent you. He will not be made into a man if he can help it.

What you would have done about that tin soldier I do not know. But what God did about us was this. The Second Person in God, the Son, became human Himself: was born into the world as an actual man—a real man of a particular height, with hair of a particular colour, speaking a particular language, weighing so many stone. The Eternal Being, who knows everything and who created the whole universe, became not only a man but (before that) a baby, and before that a foetus inside a Woman's body. If you want to get the hang of it, think how you would like to become a slug or a crab.

The result of this was that you now had one man who really was what all men were intended to be: one man in whom the created life, derived from His Mother, allowed itself to be completely and perfectly turned into the begotten life. The natural human creature in Him was taken up fully into the divine Son. Thus in one instance humanity had, so to speak, arrived: had passed into the life of Christ. And because the whole difficulty for us is that the natural life has to be, in a sense, 'killed', He chose an earthly career which involved the killing of His human desires at every turn—poverty, misunderstanding from His own family, betrayal by one of His intimate friends, being jeered at and manhandled by the Police, and execution by torture. And then, after being thus killed—killed every day in a sense—the human creature in Him, because it was united to the divine Son, came to life again. The Man in Christ rose again: not only the God. That is the whole point. For the first time we saw a real man. One tin soldier—real tin, just like the rest—had come fully and splendidly alive.

And here, of course, we come to the point where my illustration about the tin soldier breaks down. In the case of real toy soldiers or statues, if one came to life, it would obviously make no difference to the rest. They are all separate. But human beings are not. They look separate because you see them walking about separately. But then, we are so made that we can see only the present moment. If we could see the past, then of course it would look different. For there was a time when every man was part of his mother, and (earlier still) part of his father as well: and when they were part of his grandparents. If you could see humanity spread out in time, as God sees it, it would not look like a lot of separate things dotted about. It would look like one single growing thing—rather like a very complicated tree. Every individual would appear connected with every other. And not only that. Individuals are not really separate from God any more than from one another. Every man, woman, and child all over the world is feeling and breathing at this moment only because God, so to speak, is 'keeping him going'.

Consequently, when Christ becomes man it is not really as if you could become one particular tin soldier. It is as if something which is always affecting the whole human mass begins, at one point, to affect the whole human mass in a new way. From that point the effect spreads through all mankind. It makes a difference to people who lived before Christ as well as to people who lived after Him. It makes a difference to people who have never heard of Him. It is like dropping into a glass of water one drop of something which gives a new taste or a new colour to the whole lot. But, of course, none of these illustrations really works perfectly. In the long run God is no one but Himself and what He does is like nothing else. You could hardly expect it to be otherwise.

What, then, is the difference which He has made to the whole human mass? It is just this; that the business of becoming a son of God, of being turned from a created thing into a begotten thing, of passing over from the temporary biological life into timeless 'spiritual' life, has been done for us. Humanity is already 'saved' in principle. We individuals have to appropriate that salvation. But the really tough work—the bit we could not have done for ourselves—has been done for us. We have not got to try to climb up into spiritual life by our own efforts; it has already come down into the human race. If we will only lay ourselves open to the one Man in whom it was fully present, and who, in spite of being God, is also a real man, He will do it in us and for us. Remember what I said about 'good infection'. One of our own race has this new life: if we get close to Him we shall catch it from Him.

Of course, you can express this in all sorts of different ways. You can say that Christ died for our sins. You may say that the Father has forgiven us because Christ has done for us what we ought to have done. You may say that we are washed in the blood of the Lamb. You may say that Christ has defeated death. They are all true. If any of them do not appeal to you, leave it alone and get on with the formula that does. And, whatever you do, do not start quarrelling with other people because they use a different formula from yours.

MERE CHRISTIANITY
"The Obstinate Toy Soldiers"

Love's as Fierce as Fire

Scripture Readings
I John 4:7–16
Psalm 42:1–11

Love's as warm as tears,
   Love is tears:
Pressure within the brain,
Tension at the throat,
Deluge, weeks of rain,
Haystacks afloat,
Featureless seas between
Hedges, where once was green.

Love's as fierce as fire,
   Love is fire:
All sorts—infernal heat
Clinkered with greed and pride,
Lyric desire, sharp-sweet,
Laughing, even when denied,

31

And that empyreal flame
Whence all loves came.

Love's as fresh as spring,
   Love is spring:
Bird-song hung in the air,
Cool smells in a wood,
Whispering 'Dare! Dare!'
To sap, to blood,
Telling 'Ease, safety, rest,
Are good; not best.'

Love's as hard as nails,
   Love is nails:
Blunt, thick, hammered through
The medial nerves of One
Who, having made us, knew
The thing He had done,
Seeing (with all that is)
Our cross, and His.

POEMS
"Love's as Warm as Tears"

What does not satisfy when we find it, was not the thing
we were desiring. If water will not set a man at ease, then
be sure it was not thirst, or not thirst only, that tormented

him: he wanted drunkenness to cure his dullness, or talk to cure his solitude, or the like. How, indeed, do we know our desires save by their satisfaction?

When do we know them until we say, 'Ah, *this* was what I wanted'? And if there were any desire which it was natural for man to feel but impossible for man to satisfy, would not the nature of this desire remain to him always ambiguous? If old tales were true, if a man without putting off humanity could indeed pass the frontiers of our country, if he could be, and yet be a man, in that fabled East and fabled West, then indeed at the moment of fruition, the raising of the cup, the assumption of the crown, the kiss of the spouse—then first, to his backward glance, the long roads of desire that he had trodden would become plain in all their winding, and when he found, he would know what it was that he had sought. I am old and full of tears, and I see that you also begin to feel the sorrow that is born with us. Abandon hope: do not abandon desire. Feel no wonder that these glimpses of your Island so easily confuse themselves with viler things, and are so easily blasphemed. Above all, never try to keep them, never try to revisit the same place or time wherein the vision was accorded to you. You will pay the penalty of all who would bind down to one place or time within our country that which our country cannot contain. Have you not heard from the Stewards of the sin of idolatry, and how, in their old chronicles, the manna turned to worms if any tried to hoard it? Be not greedy, be not passionate; you will but crush dead on your own breast with hot, rough hands the thing you loved. But if ever you incline to doubt that the thing you long for is something real, remember what your own experience has taught you. Think that it is a *feeling*, and at once the feeling has no value. Stand sentinel at your own mind, watching for that feeling, and you will find—what shall I say?—a flutter in the heart, an image in the head, a sob in the throat: and was *that* your desire? You know that it was not, and that no feeling whatever will appease you, that *feeling*, refine it as you will, is but one more spurious claimant—spurious as the gross lusts of which the giant speaks. Let us conclude then that what you desire is no state of yourself at all, but something, for that very reason, Other and Outer. And knowing this you will find tolerable the truth that you cannot attain it. That the thing should *be*, is so great a good that when you remember 'it is' you will forget to be sorry that you can never have it. Nay, anything that you could have would be so much less than this that its fruition would be immeasurably below the mere hunger for this. Wanting is better than having. The glory of any world wherein you can live is in the end appearance: but then, as one of my sons has said, that leaves the world more glorious yet.

THE PILGRIM'S REGRESS
"Wisdom—Exoteric"

Letting Go of Fear

Scripture Readings
I Corinthians 1:26–31
Psalms 97:1–7

No. It is not Christianity which need fear the giant universe. It is those systems which place the whole meaning of existence in biological or social evolution on our own planet. It is the creative evolutionist, the Bergsonian or Shavian, or the Communist, who should tremble when he looks up at the night sky. For he really is committed to a sinking ship. He really is attempting to ignore the discovered nature of things, as though by concentrating on the possibly upward trend in a single planet he could make himself forget the inevitable downward trend in the universe as a whole, the trend to low temperatures and irrevocable disorganisation. For entropy is the real cosmic wave, and evolution only a momentary tellurian ripple within it.

On these grounds, then, I submit that we Christians

have as little to fear as anyone from the knowledge actually acquired. But, as I said at the beginning, that is not the fundamental answer. The endless fluctuations of scientific theory which seem today so much friendlier to us than in the last century may turn against us tomorrow. The basic answer lies elsewhere.

Let me remind you of the question we are trying to answer. It is this: How can an unchanging system survive the continual increase of knowledge? Now, in certain cases we know very well how it can. A mature scholar reading a great passage in Plato, and taking in at one glance the metaphysics, the literary beauty, and the place of both in the history of Europe, is in a very different position from a boy learning the Greek alphabet. Yet through that unchanging system of the alphabet all this vast mental and emotional activity is operating. It has not been broken by the new knowledge. It is not outworn. If it changed, all would be chaos. A great Christian statesman, considering the morality of a measure which will affect millions of lives, and which involves economic, geographical and political considerations of the utmost complexity, is in a different position from a boy first learning that one must not cheat or tell lies, or hurt innocent people. But only in so far as that first knowledge of the great moral platitudes survives unimpaired in the statesman will his deliberation be moral at all. If that goes, then there has been no progress, but only mere change. For change is not progress unless the core remains unchanged. A small oak grows into a big oak: if it became a beech, that would not be growth, but mere change. And thirdly, there is a great difference between counting apples and arriving at the mathematical formulae of modern physics. But the multiplication table is used in both and does not grow out of date.

In other words, wherever there is real progress in knowledge, there is some knowledge that is not superseded. Indeed, the very possibility of progress demands that there should be an unchanging element. New bottles for new wine, by all means: but not new palates, throats, and stomachs, or it would not be, for us, 'wine' at all. I take it we should all agree to find this sort of unchanging element in the simple rules of mathematics. I would add to these the primary principles of morality. And I would also add the fundamental doctrines of Christianity. To put it in rather more technical language, I claim that the positive historical statements made by Christianity have the power, elsewhere found chiefly in formal principles, of receiving, without intrinsic change, the increasing complexity of meaning which increasing knowledge puts into them.

For example, it may be true (though I don't for a moment suppose it is) that when the Nicene Creed said 'He came down from Heaven', the writers had in mind a local movement from a local heaven to the surface of the earth—like a parachute descent. Others since may have dismissed the idea of a spatial heaven altogether. But neither the significance nor the credibility of what is asserted seems to be in the least affected by the change. On either view, the thing is miraculous: on either view, the mental images which attend the act of belief are inessential. When a Central African convert and a Harley Street specialist both affirm that Christ rose from the dead, there is, no doubt, a very great difference between their thoughts. To one, the simple picture of a dead body getting up is sufficient; the other may think of a whole series of biochemical and even physical processes beginning to work backwards. The Doctor knows that, in his experience, they never have worked backwards; but the negro knows that dead bodies don't get up and walk. Both are faced with miracle, and both know it. If both think miracle impossible, the only difference is that the Doctor will expound the impossibility in much greater detail, will give an elaborate gloss on the simple statement that dead men don't walk about. If both believe, all the Doctor says will merely analyze and explicate the words 'He rose.' When the author of Genesis says that God made man in His own image, he may have pictured a vaguely corporeal God making man as a child makes a figure out of plasticine. A modern Christian philosopher may think of a process lasting from the first creation of matter to the final appearance on this planet of an organism fit to receive spiritual as well as biological life. But both mean essentially the same thing. Both are denying the same thing—the doctrine that matter by some blind power inherent in itself has produced spirituality.

GOD IN THE DOCK
"Dogma and the Universe"

The Joy of Genesis

Scripture Readings
Hebrews 12:1–13
Psalm 31:21–24

In the Space Trilogy, Lewis explores God's sovereignty of the entire universe.

What was the sense of so arranging things that anything really important should finally and absolutely depend on such a man of straw as himself? And at that moment, far away on Earth, as he now could not help remembering, men were at war, and white-faced subalterns and freckled corporals who had but lately begun to shave, stood in horrible gaps or crawled forward in deadly darkness, awaking, like him, to the preposterous truth that all really depended on their actions; and far away in time Horatius stood on the bridge, and Constantine settled in his mind whether he would or would not embrace the new religion, and Eve herself stood looking upon the forbidden fruit and the Heaven of Heavens waited for her decision. He writhed and ground his teeth, but could not help seeing. Thus, and not otherwise, the world was made. Either something or nothing must depend on individual choices. And if something, who could set bounds to it? A stone may determine the course of a river. He was that stone at this horrible moment which had become the centre of the whole universe. The eldila [super-human extraterrestrials] of all worlds, the sinless organisms of everlasting light, were silent in Deep Heaven to see what Elwin Ransom of Cambridge would do.

Then came blessed relief. He suddenly realised that he did not know what he *could* do. He almost laughed with joy. All this horror had been premature. No definite task was before him. All that was being demanded of him was a general and preliminary resolution to oppose the Enemy in any mode which circumstances might show to be desirable: in fact—and he flew back to the comforting words as a child flies back to its mother's arms—'to do his best'—or rather, to go on doing his best, for he had really been doing it all along. 'What bug-bears we make of things unnecessarily!' he murmured, settling himself in a slightly more comfortable position. A mild flood of what appeared to him to be cheerful and rational piety rose and engulfed him.

Hullo! What was this? He sat straight upright again, his heart beating wildly against his side. His thoughts had stumbled on an idea from which they started back as a man starts back when he has touched a hot poker. But this time the idea was really too childish to entertain. This time it *must* be a deception, risen from his own mind. It stood to reason that a struggle with the Devil meant a *spiritual* struggle . . . the notion of a physical combat was only fit for a savage.

PERELANDRA
Chapter 11

The Promise of Rebirth

Scripture Readings
I Peter 3:18–22
Psalm 33:13–22

In the Christian story God descends to reascend. He comes
down; down from the heights of absolute being into time
and space, down into humanity; down further still, if em-
bryologists are right, to recapitulate in the womb ancient
and pre-human phases of life; down to the very roots and
seabed of the Nature He has created. But He goes down to
come up again and bring the whole ruined world up with
Him. One has the picture of a strong man stooping lower
and lower to get himself underneath some great complicated burden. He must stoop in order to lift, he must almost
disappear under the load before he incredibly straightens
his back and marches off with the whole mass swaying on
his shoulders. Or one may think of a diver, first reducing
himself to nakedness, then glancing in mid-air, then gone
with a splash, vanished, rushing down through green and

warm water into black and cold water, down through increasing pressure into the death-like region of ooze and slime and old decay; then up again, back to colour and light, his lungs almost bursting, till suddenly he breaks surface again, holding in his hand the dripping, precious thing that he went down to recover. He and it are both coloured now that they have come up into the light: down below, where it lay colourless in the dark, he lost his colour too.

In this descent and reascent everyone will recognise a familiar pattern: a thing written all over the world. It is the pattern of all vegetable life. It must belittle itself into something hard, small and death-like, it must fall into the ground: thence the new life reascends. It is the pattern of all animal generation too. There is descent from the full and perfect organisms into the spermatozoon and ovum, and in the dark womb a life at first inferior in kind to that of the species which is being reproduced: then the slow ascent to the perfect embryo, to the living, conscious baby, and finally to the adult. So it is also in our moral and emotional life. The first innocent and spontaneous desires have to submit to the deathlike process of control or total denial: but from that there is a reascent to fully formed character in which the strength of the original material all operates but in a new way. Death and Rebirth—go down to go up—it is a key principle. Through this bottleneck, this belittlement, the highroad nearly always lies.

The doctrine of the Incarnation, if accepted, puts this

principle even more emphatically at the centre. The pattern is there in Nature because it was first there in God. All the instances of it which I have mentioned turn out to be but transpositions of the Divine theme into a minor key. I am not now referring simply to the Crucifixion and Resurrection of Christ. The total pattern, of which they are only the turning point, is the real Death and Rebirth: for certainly no seed ever fell from so fair a tree into so dark and cold a soil as would furnish more than a faint analogy to this huge descent and reascension in which God dredged the salt and oozy bottom of Creation.

From this point of view the Christian doctrine makes itself so quickly at home amid the deepest apprehensions of reality which we have from other sources, that doubt may spring up in a new direction. Is it not fitting in too well? So well that it must have come into men's minds from seeing this pattern elsewhere, particularly in the annual death and resurrection of the corn? For there have, of course, been many religions in which that annual drama (so important for the life of the tribe) was almost admittedly the central theme, and the deity—Adonis, Osiris, or another—almost undisguisedly a personification of the corn, a 'corn-king' who died and rose again each year. Is not Christ simply another corn-king?

MIRACLES
"The Grand Miracle"

The Beauty of Myths

Scripture Readings
John 1:1–14
Psalm 34:1–14

When Professor Tolkien began there was probably no nuclear fission and the contemporary incarnation of Mordor was a good deal nearer our shores. But the text itself teaches us that Sauron is eternal; the war of the Ring is only one of a thousand wars against him. Every time we shall be wise to fear his ultimate victory, after which there will be 'no more songs'. Again and again we shall have good evidence that 'the wind is setting East, and the withering of all woods may be drawing near'. Every time we win we shall know that our victory is impermanent. If we insist on asking for the moral of the story, that is its moral: a recall from facile optimism and wailing pessimism alike, to that hard, yet not quite desperate, insight into Man's unchanging predicament by which heroic ages have lived. It is here that the

Norse affinity is strongest; hammer-strokes, but with compassion.

'But why,' (some ask), 'why, if you have a serious comment to make on the real life of men, must you do it by talking about a phantasmagoric never-never land of your own?' Because, I take it, one of the main things the author wants to say is that the real life of men is of that mythical and heroic quality. One can see the principle at work in his characterisation. Much that in a realistic work would be done by 'character delineation' is here done simply by making the character an elf, a dwarf, or a hobbit. The imagined beings have their insides on the outside; they are visible souls. And Man as a whole, Man pitted against the universe, have we seen him at all till we see that he is like a hero in a fairy tale? In the book Eomer rashly contrasts 'the green earth' with 'legends'. Aragorn replies that the green earth itself is 'a mighty matter of legend'.

The value of the myth is that it takes all the things we know and restores to them the rich significance which has been hidden by 'the veil of familiarity'. The child enjoys his cold meat (otherwise dull to him) by pretending it is buffalo, just killed with his own bow and arrow. And the child is wise. The real meat comes back to him more savoury for having been dipped in a story; you might say that only then is it the real meat. If you are tired of the real landscape, look at it in a mirror. By putting bread, gold, horse, apple, or the very roads into a myth, we do not retreat from reality: we rediscover it. As long as the story lingers in our mind, the real things are more themselves. This book applies the treatment not only to bread or apple but to good and evil, to our endless perils, our anguish, and our joys. By dipping them in myth we see them more clearly. I do not think he could have done it in any other way.

ON STORIES
"Tolkien's *The Lord of the Rings*"

Through Christ We See Everything Else

Scripture Readings
Ephesians 2:1–10
Psalm 50:1–6

You remember the old puzzle as to whether the owl came from the egg or the egg from the owl. The modern acquiescence in universal evolutionism is a kind of optical illusion, produced by attending exclusively to the owl's emergence from the egg. We are taught from childhood to notice how the perfect oak grows from the acorn and to forget that the acorn itself was dropped by a perfect oak. We are reminded constantly that the adult human being was an embryo, never that the life of the embryo came from two adult human beings. We love to notice that the express engine of today is the descendant of the 'Rocket'; we do not equally remember that the 'Rocket' springs not from some even more rudimentary engine, but from something much more perfect and complicated than itself—namely, a man of genius. The obviousness or naturalness which most people seem to find in the idea of emergent evolution thus seems to be a pure hallucination.

On these grounds and others like them one is driven to think that whatever else may be true, the popular scientific cosmology at any rate is certainly not. I left that ship not at the call of poetry but because I thought it could not keep afloat. Something like philosophical idealism or Theism must, at the very worst, be less untrue than that. And idealism turned out, when you took it seriously, to be disguised Theism. And once you accepted Theism, you could not ignore the claims of Christ. And when you examined them it appeared to me that you could adopt no middle position. Either He was a lunatic, or God. And He was not a lunatic.

I was taught at school, when I had done a sum, to 'prove my answer'. The proof or verification of my Christian answer to the cosmic sum is this. When I accept Theology I may find difficulties, at this point or that, in harmonising it with some particular truths which are imbedded in the mythical cosmology derived from science. But I can get in, or allow for, science as a whole. Granted that Reason is prior to matter and that the light of that primal Reason illuminates finite minds, I can understand how men should come, by observation and inference, to know a lot about the universe they live in. If, on the other hand, I swallow the scientific cosmology as a whole, then not only can I not fit in Christianity, but I cannot even fit in science. If minds are wholly dependent on brains, and brains on biochemistry, and biochemistry (in the long run) on the meaningless flux of the atoms, I cannot understand how the thought of those minds should have any more significance than the sound of the wind in the trees. And this is to me the final test. This is how I distinguish dreaming and waking. When I am awake I can, in some degree, account for and study my dream. The dragon that pursued me last night can be fitted into my waking world. I know that there are such things as dreams; I know that I had eaten an indigestible dinner; I know that a man of my reading might be expected to dream of dragons. But while in the nightmare I could not have fitted in my waking experience. The waking world is judged more real because it can thus contain the dreaming world; the dreaming world is judged less real because it cannot contain the waking one. For the same reason I am certain that in passing from the scientific points of view to the theological, I have passed from dream to waking. Christian theology can fit in science, art, morality, and the sub-Christian religions. The scientific point of view cannot fit in any of these things, not even science itself. I believe in Christianity as I believe that the Sun has risen, not only because I see it, but because by it I see everything else.

THE WEIGHT OF GLORY
"Is Theology Poetry?"

WEEK THREE

Redefining Sin

Scripture Readings
Ephesians 1:1–10
Psalm 2:1–12

Jesus asks those at the well who are sinless to cast the first stone. Paul says we have all fallen short and missed the mark. Let's not gloss over our corruption but rather recognize it and confess it. Remember that he is faithful and just to forgive us and cleanse us from all unrighteousness.

I JOHN 1:9

A recovery of the old sense of sin is essential to Christianity. Christ takes it for granted that men are bad. Until we really feel this assumption of His to be true, though we are part of the world He came to save, we are not part of the audience to whom His words are addressed. We lack the first condition for understanding what He is talking about. And when men attempt to be Christians without this preliminary consciousness of sin, the result is almost bound to be a certain resentment against God as to one always inexplicably angry. Most of us have at times felt a secret sympathy with the dying farmer who replied to the Vicar's dissertation on repentance by asking 'What harm have I ever done *Him*?' There is the real rub. The worst we have done to God is to leave Him alone—why can't He return the compliment? Why not live and let live? What call has He, of all beings, to be 'angry'? It's easy for Him to be good!

Now at the moment when a man feels real guilt—moments too rare in our lives—all these blasphemies vanish away. Much, we may feel, can be excused to human infirmities: but not *this*—this incredibly mean and ugly action which none of our friends would have done, which even such a thorough-going little rotter as X would have been ashamed of, which we would not for the world allow to be published. At such a moment we really do know that our character, as revealed in this action, is, and ought to be, hateful to all good men, and, if there are powers above man, to them. A God who did not regard this with unappeasable distaste would not be a good being. We cannot even wish for such a God—it is like wishing that every nose in the universe were abolished, that smell of hay or roses or the sea should never again delight any creature, because our own breath happens to stink.

When we merely *say* that we are bad, the 'wrath' of God seems a barbarous doctrine; as soon as we *perceive* our badness, it appears inevitable, a mere corollary from God's goodness. To keep ever before us the insight derived from such a moment as I have been describing, to learn to detect the same real inexcusable corruption under more and more of its complex disguises, is therefore indispensable to a real understanding of the Christian faith. This is not, of course, a new doctrine. I am attempting nothing very splendid. . . . I am merely trying to get my reader (and, still more, myself) over a *pons asinorum*—to take the first step out of fools' paradise and utter illusion.

THE PROBLEM OF PAIN
"Human Wickedness"

Longing for Heaven

Scripture Readings
I Corinthians 1:20–25
Psalm 74:12–17

Hope is one of the Theological virtues. This means that a continual looking forward to the eternal world is not (as some modern people think) a form of escapism or wishful thinking, but one of the things a Christian is meant to do. It does not mean that we are to leave the present world as it is. If you read history you will find that the Christians who did most for the present world were just those who thought most of the next. The Apostles themselves, who set on foot the conversion of the Roman Empire, the great men who built up the Middle Ages, the English Evangelicals who abolished the Slave Trade, all left their mark on Earth, precisely because their minds were occupied with Heaven. It is since Christians have largely ceased to think of the other world that they have become so ineffective in this. Aim at Heaven and you will get earth 'thrown in': aim at earth and you will get neither. It seems a strange rule, but something like it can be seen at work in other matters. Health is a great blessing, but the moment you make health one of your main, direct objects you start becoming a crank and imagining there is something wrong with you. You are only likely to get health provided you want other things more—food, games, work, fun, open air. In the same way, we shall never save civilisation as long as civilisation is our main object. We must learn to want something else even more.

Most of us find it very difficult to want 'Heaven' at all—except in so far as 'Heaven' means meeting again our friends who have died. One reason for this difficulty is that we have not been trained: our whole education tends to fix our minds on this world. Another reason is that when the real want for Heaven is present in us, we do not recognise it. Most people, if they had really learned to look into their own hearts, would know that they do want, and want acutely, something that cannot be had in this world. There are all sorts of things in this world that offer to give it to you, but they never quite keep their promise. The longings which arise in us when we first fall in love, or first think of some foreign country, or first take up some subject that excites us, are longings which no marriage, no travel, no learning, can really satisfy. I am not now speaking of what would be ordinarily called unsuccessful marriages, or holidays, or learned careers. I am speaking of the best possible ones. There was something we grasped at, in that first moment of longing, which just fades away in the reality. I think everyone knows what I mean. The wife may be a good wife, and the hotels and scenery may have been excellent, and chemistry may be a very interesting job: but something has evaded us. Now there are two wrong ways of dealing with this fact, and one right one.

(1) The Fool's Way—He puts the blame on the things themselves. He goes on all his life thinking that if only he tried another woman, or went for a more expensive holiday, or whatever it is, then, this time, he really would catch the mysterious something we are all after. Most of the bored, discontented, rich people in the world are of this type. They spend their whole lives trotting from woman to woman (through the divorce courts), from continent to continent, from hobby to hobby, always thinking that the latest is 'the Real Thing' at last, and always disappointed.

(2) The Way of the Disillusioned 'Sensible Man'—He soon decides that the whole thing was moonshine. 'Of course,' he says, 'one feels like that when one's young. But by the time you get to my age you've given up chasing the rainbow's end.' And so he settles down and learns not to expect too much and represses the part of himself which used, as he would say, 'to cry for the moon'. This is, of course, a much better way than the first, and makes

a man much happier, and less of a nuisance to society. It tends to make him a prig (he is apt to be rather superior towards what he calls 'adolescents'), but, on the whole, he rubs along fairly comfortably. It would be the best line we could take if man did not live forever. But supposing infinite happiness really is there, waiting for us? Supposing one really can reach the rainbow's end? In that case it would be a pity to find out too late (a moment after death) that by our supposed 'common sense' we had stifled in ourselves the faculty of enjoying it.

(3) The Christian Way—The Christian says, 'Creatures are not born with desires unless satisfaction for those desires exists. A baby feels hunger: well, there is such a thing as food. A duckling wants to swim: well, there is such a thing as water. Men feel sexual desire: well, there is such a thing as sex. If I find in myself a desire which no experience in this world can satisfy, the most probable explanation is that I was made for another world. If none of my earthly pleasures satisfy it, that does not prove that the universe is a fraud. Probably earthly pleasures were never meant to satisfy it, but only to arouse it, to suggest the real thing. If that is so, I must take care, on the one hand, never to despise, or be unthankful for, these earthly blessings, and on the other, never to mistake them for the something else of which they are only a kind of copy, or echo, or mirage. I must keep alive in myself the desire for my true country, which I shall not

find till after death; I must never let it get snowed under or turned aside; I must make it the main object of life to press on to that other country and to help others to do the same.'

There is no need to be worried by facetious people who try to make the Christian hope of 'Heaven' ridiculous by saying they do not want 'to spend eternity playing harps'. The answer to such people is that if they cannot understand books written for grown-ups, they should not talk about them. All the scriptural imagery (harps, crowns, gold, etc.) is, of course, a merely symbolical attempt to express the inexpressible. Musical instruments are mentioned because for many people (not all) music is the thing known in the present life which most strongly suggests ecstasy and infinity. Crowns are mentioned to suggest the fact that those who are united with God in eternity share His splendour and power and joy. Gold is mentioned to suggest the timelessness of Heaven (gold does not rust) and the preciousness of it. People who take these symbols literally might as well think that when Christ told us to be like doves, He meant that we were to lay eggs.

MERE CHRISTIANITY
"Hope"

God's Medicine

Scripture Readings
Jeremiah 31:31–34
Psalm 19:1–6

So much for the sense in which human Death is the result of sin and the triumph of Satan. But it is also the means of redemption from sin, God's medicine for Man and His weapon against Satan. In a general way it is not difficult to understand how the same thing can be a masterstroke on the part of one combatant and also the very means whereby the superior combatant defeats him. Every good general, every good chess-player, takes what is precisely the strong point of his opponent's plan and makes it the pivot of his own plan. Take that castle of mine if you insist. It was not my original intention that you should—indeed, I thought you would have had more sense. But take it by all means. For now I move thus . . . and thus . . . and it is mate in three moves. Something like this must be supposed to have happened about Death. Do not say that such metaphors are too trivial to illustrate so high a matter: the unnoticed mechanical and mineral metaphors which, in this age, will dominate our whole minds (without being recognised as metaphors at all) the moment we relax our vigilance against them, must be incomparably less adequate.

And one can see how it might have happened. The Enemy persuades Man to rebel against God: Man, by doing so, loses power to control that other rebellion which the Enemy now raises in Man's organism (both psychical and physical) against Man's spirit: just as that organism, in its turn, loses power to maintain itself against the rebellion of the inorganic. In that way, Satan produced human Death. But when God created Man he gave him such a constitution that, if the highest part of it rebelled against Himself, it would be bound to lose control over the lower parts: i.e., in the long run to suffer Death. This provision may be regarded equally as a punitive sentence ('In the day ye eat of that fruit ye shall die'), as a mercy, and as a safety device. It is punishment because Death—that Death of which Martha says to Christ 'But . . . Sir . . . it'll *smell*'—is horror and ignominy. ('I am not so much afraid of death as ashamed of it,' said Sir Thomas Browne.) It is mercy because by willing and humble surrender to it Man undoes his act of rebellion and makes even this depraved and monstrous mode of Death an instance of that higher and mystical

Death which is eternally good and a necessary ingredient in the highest life. 'The readiness is all'—not, of course, the merely heroic readiness but that of humility and self-renunciation. Our enemy, so welcomed, becomes our servant: bodily Death, the monster, becomes blessed spiritual Death to self, if the spirit so wills—or rather if it allows the Spirit of the willingly dying God so to will in it. It is a safety-device because, once Man has fallen, natural immortality would be the one utterly hopeless destiny for him. Aided to the surrender that he must make by no external necessity of Death, free (if you call it freedom) to rivet faster and faster about himself through unending centuries the chains of his own pride and lust and of the nightmare civilisations which these build up in ever-increasing power and complication, he would progress from being merely a fallen man to being a fiend, possibly beyond all modes of redemption. This danger was averted. The sentence that those who ate of the forbidden fruit would be driven away from the Tree of Life was implicit in the composite nature with which Man was created. But to convert this penal death into the means of eternal life—to add to its negative and preventive function a positive and saving function—it was further necessary that death should be *accepted*. Humanity must embrace death freely, submit to it with total humility, drink it to the dregs, and so convert it into that mystical death which is the secret of life. But only a Man who did not need to have been a Man at all unless He had chosen, only one who served in our sad regiment as a volunteer, yet also only one who was perfectly a Man, could perform this perfect dying; and thus (which way you put it is unimportant) either defeat death or redeem it. He tasted death on behalf of all others. He is the representative 'Die-er' of the universe: and for that very reason the Resurrection and the Life. Or conversely, because He truly lives, He truly dies, for that is the very pattern of reality. Because the higher can descend into the lower He who from all eternity has been incessantly plunging Himself in the blessed death of self-surrender to the Father can also most fully descend into the horrible and (for us) involuntary death of the body. Because Vicariousness is the very idiom of the reality He has created, His death can become ours. The whole Miracle, far from denying what we already know of reality, writes the comment which makes that crabbed text plain: or rather, proves itself to be the text on which Nature was only the commentary. In science we have been reading only the notes to a poem; in Christianity we find the poem itself.

MIRACLES
"The Grand Miracle"

The Promise of Forgiveness

Scripture Readings
I John 1:5–10
Psalm 19:7–14

We say a great many things in church (and out of church too) without thinking of what we are saying. For instance, we say in the Creed 'I believe in the forgiveness of sins.' I had been saying it for several years before I asked myself why it was in the Creed. At first sight it seems hardly worth putting in. 'If one is a Christian,' I thought, 'of course one believes in the forgiveness of sins. It goes without saying.' But the people who compiled the Creed apparently thought that this was a part of our belief which we needed to be reminded of every time we went to church. And I have begun to see that, as far as I am concerned, they were right. To believe in the forgiveness of sins is not nearly so easy as I thought. Real belief in it is the sort of thing that very easily slips away if we don't keep on polishing it up.

We believe that God forgives us our sins; but also that He will not do so unless we forgive other people their sins against us. There is no doubt about the second part of this statement. It is in the Lord's Prayer; it was emphatically stated by our Lord. If you don't forgive you will not be forgiven. No part of His teaching is clearer, and there are no exceptions to it. He doesn't say that we are to forgive other people's sins provided they are not too frightful, or provided there are extenuating circumstances, or anything of that sort. We are to forgive them all, however spiteful, however mean, however often they are repeated. If we don't, we shall be forgiven none of our own.

Now it seems to me that we often make a mistake both about God's forgiveness of our sins and about the forgiveness we are told to offer to other people's sins. Take it first about God's forgiveness. I find that when I think I am asking God to forgive me I am often in reality (unless I watch myself very carefully) asking Him to do something quite different. I am asking Him not to forgive me but to excuse me. But there is all the difference in the world between forgiving and excusing. Forgiveness says, 'Yes, you have done this thing, but I accept your apology; I will never hold it against you and everything between us two will be exactly as it was before.' But excusing says, 'I see that you couldn't help it or didn't mean it; you weren't really to blame.' If one was not really to blame then there is nothing to forgive. In that sense forgiveness and excusing are almost opposites. Of course, in dozens of cases, either between God and man, or between one man and another, there may be a mixture of the two. Part of what seemed at first to be the sins turns out to be really nobody's fault and is excused; the bit that is left over is forgiven. If you had a perfect excuse, you would not need forgiveness; if the whole of your action needs forgiveness, then there was no excuse for it. But the trouble is that what we call 'asking God's forgiveness' very often really consists in asking God to accept our excuses. What leads us into this mistake is the fact that there usually is some amount of excuse, some 'extenuating circumstances'. We are so very anxious to point these out to God (and to ourselves) that we are apt to forget the really important thing; that is, the bit left over, the bit which the excuses don't cover, the bit which is inexcusable but not, thank God, unforgivable. And if we forget this, we shall go away imagining that we have repented and been forgiven when all that has really happened is that we have satisfied ourselves with our own excuses. They may be very bad excuses; we are all too easily satisfied about ourselves.

There are two remedies for this danger. One is to remember that God knows all the real excuses very much better than we do. If there are real 'extenuating circumstances' there is no fear that He will overlook them. Often He must know many excuses that we have never thought of, and therefore humble souls will, after death, have the delightful surprise of discovering that on certain occasions they sinned much less than they had thought. All the real excusing He will do. What we have got to take to Him is the inexcusable bit, the sin. We are only wasting time by talking about all the parts which can (we think) be excused. When you go to a doctor you show him the bit of you that is wrong—say, a broken arm. It would be a mere waste of time to keep on explaining that your legs and eyes and throat are all right. You may be mistaken in thinking so, and anyway, if they are really all right, the doctor will know that.

The second remedy is really and truly to believe in the forgiveness of sins. A great deal of our anxiety to make excuses comes from not really believing in it, from thinking that God will not take us to Himself again unless He is satisfied that some sort of case can be made out in our favour. But that would not be forgiveness at all. Real forgiveness means looking steadily at the sin, the sin that is left over without any excuse, after all allowances have been made, and seeing it in all its horror, dirt, meanness, and malice, and nevertheless being wholly reconciled to the man who has done it. That, and only that, is forgiveness, and that we can always have from God if we ask for it.

THE WEIGHT OF GLORY
"On Forgiveness"

70

The Three Kinds of People

Scripture Readings
Luke 21:1–19
Psalm 102:1–11

There are three kinds of people in the world. The first class is of those who live simply for their own sake and pleasure, regarding Man and Nature as so much raw material to be cut up into whatever shape may serve them. In the second class are those who acknowledge some other claim upon them—the will of God, the categorical imperative, or the good of society—and honestly try to pursue their own interests no further than this claim will allow. They try to surrender to the higher claim as much as it demands, like men paying a tax, but hope, like other taxpayers, that what is left over will be enough for them to live on. Their life is divided, like a soldier's or a schoolboy's life, into time 'on parade' and 'off parade', 'in school' and 'out of school'. But the third class is of those who can say like St Paul that for them 'to live is Christ'. These people have got rid of the tiresome business of adjusting the rival claims of Self and God by the simple expedient of rejecting the claims of Self altogether. The old egoistic will has been turned round, reconditioned, and made into a new thing. The will of Christ no longer limits theirs; it is theirs. All their time, in belonging to Him, belongs also to them, for they are His.

And because there are three classes, any merely twofold division of the world into good and bad is disastrous. It overlooks the fact that the members of the second class (to which most of us belong) are always and necessarily unhappy. The tax which moral conscience levies on our desires does not in fact leave us enough to live on. As long as we are in this class we must either feel guilt because we have not paid the tax or penury because we have. The Christian doctrine that there is no 'salvation' by works done according to the moral law is a fact of daily experience. Back or on we must go. But there is no going on simply by our own efforts. If the new Self, the new Will, does not come at His own good pleasure to be born in us, we cannot produce Him synthetically.

The price of Christ is something, in a way, much easier than moral effort—it is to want Him. It is true that the wanting itself would be beyond our power but for one fact. The world is so built that, to help us desert our own satisfactions, they desert us. War and trouble and finally old age take from us one by one all those things that the natural Self hoped for at its setting out. Begging is our only wisdom, and want in the end makes it easier for us to be beggars. Even on those terms the Mercy will receive us.

PRESENT CONCERNS
"Three Kinds of Men"

An Invitation to Divine Ecstasy

Scripture Readings
Romans 8:26–39
Psalm 44:20–26

*Lewis was a medieval literature scholar, and today's reading is
from one of his books on that time period.*

Theologically, Protestantism was either a recovery, or
a development, or an exaggeration (it is not for the literary historian to say which) of Pauline theology. . . .
In the mind of a Tyndale or Luther, as in the mind of
St Paul himself, this theology was by no means an intellectual construction made in the interests of speculative
thought. It springs directly out of a highly specialized
religious experience; and all its affirmations, when separated from that context, become meaningless or else
mean the opposite of what was intended.

Propositions originally framed with the sole purpose
of praising the Divine compassion as boundless, hardly

credible, and utterly gratuitous, build up, when extrapolated and systematized, into something that sounds not unlike devil-worship. The experience is that of catastrophic conversion. The man who has passed through it feels like one who has waked from nightmare into ecstasy. Like an accepted lover, he feels that he has done nothing, and never could have done anything, to deserve such astonishing happiness. Never again can he 'crow from the dunghill of desert'. All the initiative has been on God's side; all has been free, unbounded grace. And all will continue to be free, unbounded grace. His own puny and ridiculous efforts would be as helpless to retain the joy as they would have been to achieve it in the first place. Fortunately they need not. Bliss is not for sale, cannot be earned. 'Works' have no 'merit', though of course faith, inevitably, even unconsciously, flows out into works of love at once. He is not saved because he does works of love: he does works of love because he is saved. It is faith alone that has saved him: faith bestowed by sheer gift. From this buoyant humility, this farewell to the self with all its good resolutions, anxiety, scruples, and motive-scratchings, all the Protestant doctrines originally sprang.

For it must be clearly understood that they were at first doctrines not of terror but of joy and hope: indeed, more than hope, fruition, for as Tyndale says, the converted man is already tasting eternal life. The doctrine of predestination, says the XVIIth Article, is 'full of sweet, pleasant and unspeakable comfort to godly persons'. But what of ungodly persons? Inside the original experience no such question arises. There are no generalisations. We are not building a system. When we begin to do so, very troublesome problems and very dark solutions will appear. But these horrors, so familiar to the modern reader (and especially to the modern reader of fiction), are only by-products of the new theology. They are astonishingly absent from the thought of the first Protestants. Relief and buoyancy are the characteristic notes. In a single sentence of the *Tischreden* Luther tosses the question aside forever. Do you doubt whether you are elected to salvation? Then say your prayers, man, and you may conclude that you are. It is as easy as that.

ENGLISH LITERATURE IN THE SIXTEENTH
CENTURY EXCLUDING DRAMA
pages 33–34

God's Joy Is Our Joy

Scripture Readings
Hebrews 2:5–11
Psalm 8:1–9

God made us: invented us as a man invents an engine. A car is made to run on petrol, and it would not run properly on anything else. Now God designed the human machine to run on Himself. He Himself is the fuel our spirits were designed to burn, or the food our spirits were designed to feed on. There is no other. That is why it is just no good asking God to make us happy in our own way without bothering about religion. God cannot give us a happiness and peace apart from Himself, because it is not there. There is no such thing.

That is the key to history. Terrific energy is expended—civilisations are built up—excellent institutions devised; but each time something goes wrong. Some fatal flaw always brings the selfish and cruel people to the top and it all slides back into misery and ruin. In fact, the machine conks. It seems to start up all right and runs a few yards, and then it breaks down. They are trying to run it on the wrong juice. That is what Satan has done to us humans.

And what did God do? First of all He left us conscience, the sense of right and wrong: and all through history there have been people trying (some of them very hard) to obey it. None of them ever quite succeeded. Secondly, He sent the human race what I call good dreams: I mean those queer stories scattered all through the heathen religions about a god who dies and comes to life again and, by his death, has somehow given new life to men. Thirdly, He selected one particular people and spent several centuries hammering into their heads the sort of God He was—that there was only one of Him and that He cared about right conduct. Those people were the Jews, and the Old Testament gives an account of the hammering process.

Then comes the real shock. Among these Jews there suddenly turns up a man who goes about talking as if He was God. He claims to forgive sins. He says He has always existed. He says He is coming to judge the world at the end of time. Now let us get this clear. Among Pantheists, like the Indians, anyone might say that he was a part of God, or one with God: there would be nothing very odd about it. But this man, since He was a Jew, could not mean that kind of God. God, in their language, meant the Being outside the world, who had made it and was infinitely different from anything else. And when you have grasped that, you will see that what this man said was, quite simply, the most shocking thing that has ever been uttered by human lips.

One part of the claim tends to slip past us unnoticed because we have heard it so often that we no longer see what it amounts to. I mean the claim to forgive sins: any sins. Now unless the speaker is God, this is really so preposterous as to be comic. We can all understand how a man forgives offences against himself. You tread on my toes and I forgive you, you steal my money and I forgive you. But what should we make of a man, himself unrobbed and untrodden on, who announced that he forgave you for treading on other men's toes and stealing other men's money? Asinine fatuity is the kindest description we should give of his conduct. Yet this is what Jesus did. He told people that their sins were forgiven, and never waited to consult all the other people whom their sins had undoubtedly injured. He unhesitatingly behaved as if He was the party chiefly concerned, the person chiefly offended in all offences. This makes sense only if He really was the God whose laws are broken and whose love is wounded in every sin. In the mouth of any speaker who is not God, these words would imply what I can only regard as a silliness and conceit unrivalled by any other character in history.

MERE CHRISTIANITY
"The Shocking Alternative"

WEEK FOUR

Imaginative Prayer

Scripture Readings
Mark 8:34–9:1
Psalm 91:1–8

There is indeed one mental image which does not lure me away into trivial elaborations. I mean the Crucifixion itself; not seen in terms of all the pictures and crucifixes, but as we must suppose it to have been in its raw, historical reality. But even this is of less spiritual value than one might expect. Compunction, compassion, gratitude—all the fruitful emotions—are strangled. Sheer physical horror leaves no room for them. Nightmare. Even so, the image ought to be periodically faced. But no one could live with it. It did not become a frequent motif of Christian art until the generations which had seen real crucifixions were all dead. As for many hymns and sermons on the subject—endlessly harping on blood, as if that were all that mattered—they must be the work either of people so far above me that they can't reach me, or else of people with no imagination at all. (Some might be cut off from me by both these gulfs.)

Yet mental images play an important part in my prayers. I doubt if any act of will or thought or emotion occurs in me without them. But they seem to help me most when they are most fugitive and fragmentary—rising and bursting like bubbles in champagne or wheeling like rooks in a windy sky: contradicting one another (in logic) as the crowded metaphors of a swift poet may do. Fix on any one, and it goes dead. You must do as Blake would do with a joy; kiss it as it flies. And then, in their total effect, they do mediate to me something very important. It is always something qualitative—more like an adjective than a noun. That, for me, gives it the impact of reality. For I think we respect nouns (and what we think they stand for) too much. All my deepest, and certainly all my earliest, experiences seem to be of sheer quality. The terrible and the lovely are older and solider than terrible and lovely things. If a musical phrase could be translated into words at all it would become an adjective. A great lyric is very like a long, utterly adequate, adjective. Plato was not so silly as the Moderns think when he elevated abstract nouns—that is, adjectives disguised as nouns—into the supreme realities—the Forms.

I know very well that in logic God is a 'substance'. Yet my thirst for quality is authorised even here: 'We give thanks to thee for thy great glory.' He *is* this glory. What

He is (the quality) is no abstraction from Him. A personal God, to be sure; but so much more than personal. To speak more soberly, our whole distinction between 'things' and 'qualities', 'substances' and 'attitudes', has no application to Him. Perhaps it has much less than we suppose even to the created universe. Perhaps it is only part of the stage set.

The wave of images, thrown off like a spray from the prayer, all momentary, all correcting, refining, 'interanimating' one another, and giving a kind of spiritual body to the unimaginable, occurs more, I find, in acts of worship than in petitionary prayers. Of which, perhaps, we have written enough. But I don't regret it. They are the right starting point. They raise all the problems. If anyone attempted to practise, or to discuss, the higher forms without going through this turnstile, I should distrust him. 'The higher does not stand without the lower.' An omission or disdain of petitionary prayer can sometimes, I think, spring not from superior sanctity but from a lack of faith and a consequent preference for levels where the question: 'Am I only doing things to myself?' does not jut out in such apparent crudity.

LETTERS TO MALCOLM, CHIEFLY ON PRAYER
Chapter 16

The Glory in All We Do

Scripture Readings
Romans 8:26–34
Psalm 91:9–16

God's claim is infinite and inexorable. You can refuse it, or you can begin to try to grant it. There is no middle way. Yet in spite of this it is clear that Christianity does not exclude any of the ordinary human activities. St Paul tells people to get on with their jobs. He even assumes that Christians may go to dinner parties, and, what is more, dinner parties given by pagans. Our Lord attends a wedding and provides miraculous wine. Under the aegis of His Church, and in the most Christian ages, learning and the arts flourish. The solution of this paradox is, of course, well known to you. 'Whether ye eat or drink or whatsoever ye do, do all to the glory of God.'

All our merely natural activities will be accepted, if they are offered to God, even the humblest, and all of them, even the noblest, will be sinful if they are not. Christianity does not simply replace our natural life and substitute a new one; it is rather a new organisation which exploits, to its own supernatural ends, these natural materials. No doubt, in a given situation, it demands the surrender of some, or of all, our merely human pursuits; it is better to be saved with one eye, than, having two, to be cast into Gehenna. But it does this, in a sense, *per accidens*—because, in those special circumstances, it has ceased to be possible to practise this or that activity to the glory of God. There is no essential quarrel between the spiritual life and the human activities as such. Thus the omnipresence of obedience to God in a Christian's life is, in a way, analogous to the omnipresence of God in space. God does not fill space as a body fills it, in the sense that parts of Him are in different parts of space, excluding other objects from them. Yet He is everywhere—totally present at every point of space—according to good theologians.

We are now in a position to answer the view that human culture is an inexcusable frivolity on the part of creatures loaded with such awful responsibilities as we. I reject at once an idea which lingers in the mind of some modern people that cultural activities are in their own right spiritual and meritorious—as though scholars and poets were intrinsically more pleasing to God than scavengers and bootblacks. I think it was Matthew Arnold who first used the English word *spiritual* in the sense of the German *geistlich,* and so inaugurated this most dangerous and most anti-Christian error. Let us clear it forever from our minds. The work of a Beethoven and the work of a charwoman become spiritual on precisely the same condition, that of being offered to God, of being done humbly 'as to the Lord'. This does not, of course, mean that it is for anyone a mere toss-up whether he should sweep rooms or compose symphonies. A mole must dig to the glory of God and a cock must crow. We are members of one body, but differentiated members, each with his own vocation. A man's upbringing, his talents, his circumstances, are usually a tolerable index of his vocation. If our parents have sent us to Oxford, if our country allows us to remain there, this is *prima facie* evidence that the life which we, at any rate, can best lead to the glory of God at present is the learned life. By leading that life to the glory of God I do not, of course, mean any attempt to make our intellectual inquiries work out to edifying conclusions. That would be, as Bacon says, to offer to the author of truth the unclean sacrifice of a lie. I mean the pursuit of knowledge and beauty, in a sense, for their own sake, but in a sense which does not exclude their being for God's sake. An appetite for these things exists in the human mind, and God makes no appetite in vain. We can therefore pursue knowledge as such, and beauty as such, in the sure confidence that by so doing we are either advancing to the vision of God ourselves or indirectly helping others to do so.

THE WEIGHT OF GLORY
"Learning in War-Time"

The Beauty of Vulnerable Love

Scripture Readings
Ephesians 5:1–6
Psalm 5:5–12

There is no safe investment. To love at all is to be vulnerable. Love anything, and your heart will certainly be wrung and possibly be broken. If you want to make sure of keeping it intact, you must give your heart to no one, not even to an animal. Wrap it carefully round with hobbies and little luxuries; avoid all entanglements; lock it up safe in the casket or coffin of your selfishness. But in that casket—safe, dark, motionless, airless—it will change. It will not be broken; it will become unbreakable, impenetrable, irredeemable. The alternative to tragedy, or at least to the risk of tragedy, is damnation. The only place outside Heaven where you can be perfectly safe from all the dangers and perturbations of love is Hell.

I believe that the most lawless and inordinate loves are less contrary to God's will than a self-invited and self-protective lovelessness. It is like hiding the talent in a napkin and for much the same reason. 'I knew thee that thou wert a hard man.' Christ did not teach and suffer that we might become, even in the natural loves, more careful of our own happiness. If a man is not uncalculating towards the earthly beloveds whom he has seen, he is none the more likely to be so towards God whom he has not. We shall draw nearer to God, not by trying to avoid the sufferings inherent in all loves, but by accepting them and offering them to Him; throwing away all defensive armour. If our hearts need to be broken, and if He chooses this as the way in which they should break, so be it.

It remains certainly true that all natural loves can be inordinate. *Inordinate* does not mean 'insufficiently cautious'. Nor does it mean 'too big'. It is not a quantitative term. It is probably impossible to love any human being simply 'too much'. We may love him too much *in proportion to* our love for God; but it is the smallness of our love for God, not the greatness of our love for the man, that constitutes the inordinacy. But even this must be refined upon. Otherwise we shall trouble some who are very much on the right road but alarmed because they cannot feel towards God so warm a sensible emotion as they feel for the earthly Beloved. It is much to be wished—at least I think so—that we all, at all times, could. We must pray that this gift should be given us. But the question whether we are loving God or the earthly Beloved 'more' is not, so far as concerns our Christian duty, a question about the comparative intensity of two feelings. The real question is, which (when the alternative comes) do you serve, or choose, or put first? To which claim does your will, in the last resort, yield?

As so often, Our Lord's own words are both far fiercer and far more tolerable than those of the theologians. He says nothing about guarding against earthly loves for fear we might be hurt; He says something that cracks like a whip about trampling them all under foot the moment they hold us back from following Him. 'If any man come to me and hate not his father and mother and wife . . . and his own life also, he cannot be my disciple' (Luke 14:26).

THE FOUR LOVES
"Charity"

On the Dark Questions

Scripture Readings
Isaiah 56:1–7
Psalm 27:4–9

Lewis spent considerable time responding to letters. This is a reply to a Mrs. Johnson where he answered a series of questions she presented.

'Do people get another chance after death? I refer to Charles Williams.'

Distinguish (A) A second chance in the strict sense, i.e., a new earthly life in which you would attempt afresh all the problems you failed at in the present one (as in religions of Re-Incarnation). (B) Purgatory: a process by which the work of redemption continues, and first perhaps begins to be noticeable after death. I think Charles Williams depicts B, not A.

'What would happen if I had died an atheist?'

We are never given any knowledge of 'What would have happened if . . .'

'What happens to Jews who are still waiting for the Messiah?'

I think that every prayer which is sincerely made even to a false god or to a very imperfectly conceived true God, is accepted by the true God and that Christ saves many who do not think they know Him. For He is (dimly) present in the *good* side of the inferior teachers they follow. In the parable of the Sheep and the Goats (Matt. 25:31 and following) those who are saved do not seem to know that they have served Christ. But of course our anxiety about unbelievers is most usefully employed when it leads us not to speculation but to earnest prayer for them and the attempt to be in our own lives such good advertisements for Christianity as will make it attractive.

'Is the Bible infallible?'

It is Christ Himself, not the Bible, who is the true word of God. The Bible, read in the right spirit and with the guidance of good teachers will bring us to Him. When it becomes really necessary (i.e., for our spiritual life, not for controversy or curiosity) to know whether a particular passage is rightly translated or is myth (but of course myth specially chosen by God from among countless myths to carry a spiritual truth) or history, we shall no doubt be guided to the right answer. But we must not use the Bible (our fathers too often did) as a sort of Encyclopedia out of which texts (isolated from their context and not read without attention to the whole nature and purport of the books in which they occur) can be taken for use as weapons.

'If a thief killed Eileen would I be wrong to want him to die?'

The question of what you wd. 'want' is off the point. Capital punishment might be wrong tho' the relations of the murdered man wanted him killed: it might be right tho' they did not want this. The question is whether a Xtian nation ought or ought not to put murderers to death: not what passions interested individuals may feel.

'Is killing in self defense all right?'

There is no doubt at all that the natural impulse to 'hit back' must be fought against by the Xtian whenever it arises. If one I love is tortured or murdered my desire to avenge him must be given no quarter. So far as nothing but this question of retaliation comes in 'turn the other cheek' is the Christian law. It is, however, quite another matter when the neutral, public authority (*not* the aggrieved person) may order killing of either private murderers or public enemies in mass. It is quite clear that our earliest Christian writer, St Paul, approved of capital punishment—he says 'the magistrate bears and should bear the sword'. It is recorded that the soldiers who came to St John Baptist asking, 'What shall we do?' were *not* told to leave the army. When Our Lord Himself praised the Centurion He never hinted that the military profession was in itself sinful. This has been the general view

of Christendom. Pacifism is a v. recent and local varia-
tion. We must of course respect and tolerate Pacifists, but
I think their view erroneous.

'Will we recognize our loved ones in Heaven?'

The symbols under which Heaven is presented to us
are (a) a dinner party, (b) a wedding, (c) a city, and (d)
a concert. It wd. be grotesque to suppose that the guests
or citizens or members of the choir didn't know one another. And how can love of one another be commanded
in this life if it is to be cut short at death?

'If Wayne didn't go to Heaven I wouldn't want to either.
Would his name be erased from my brain?'

Whatever the answer is, I'm sure it is not that ('erased
from the brain'). When I have learnt to love God better
than my earthly dearest, I shall love my earthly dearest better than I do now. In so far as I learn to love my
earthly dearest at the expense of God and *instead* of God,
I shall be moving towards the state in which I shall not
love my earthly dearest at all. When first things are put
first, second things are not suppressed but increased. If
you and I ever come to love God perfectly, the answer
to this tormenting question will then become clear, and
will be far more beautiful than we cd. ever imagine. We
can't have it now.

THE COLLECTED LETTERS OF C. S. LEWIS
Volume III, 8 November 1952

Examining Ideas of Heaven from Other Faiths

Scripture Readings
John 14:1–7
Psalm 139:7–12

In reading about ancient Egypt one gets the impression of a culture in which the main business of life was the attempt to secure the well-being of the dead. It looks as if God did not want the chosen people to follow that example. We may ask why. Is it possible for men to be too much concerned with their eternal destiny? In one sense, paradoxical though it sounds, I should reply, Yes.

For the truth seems to me to be that happiness or misery beyond death, simply in themselves, are not even religious subjects at all. A man who believes in them will of course be prudent to seek the one and avoid the other. But that seems to have no more to do with religion than looking after one's health or saving money for one's old age. The only difference here is that the stakes are so very much higher. And this means that, granted a real and steady conviction, the hopes and anxieties aroused are overwhelming. But they are not on that account the more religious. They are hopes for oneself, anxieties for oneself. God is not in the centre. He is still important only for the sake of something else. Indeed such a belief can exist without a belief in God at all. Buddhists are much concerned with what will happen to them after death, but are not, in any true sense, Theists.

It is surely, therefore, very possible that when God began to reveal Himself to men, to show them that He and nothing else is their true goal and the satisfaction of their needs, and that He has a claim upon them simply by being what He is, quite apart from anything He can bestow or deny, it may have been absolutely necessary that this revelation should not begin with any hint of future Beatitude or Perdition. These are not the right point to begin at. An effective belief in them, coming too soon, may even render almost impossible the development of (so to call it) the appetite for God; personal hopes and fears, too obviously exciting, have got in first. Later, when, after centuries of spiritual training, men have learned to desire and adore God, to pant after Him 'as pants the hart', it is another matter. For then those who love God will desire not only to enjoy Him but 'to enjoy Him forever', and will fear to lose Him. And it is by that door that a truly religious hope of Heaven and fear of Hell can enter; as corollaries to a faith already centred upon God, not as things of any independent or intrinsic weight. It is even arguable that the moment 'Heaven' ceases to mean union with God and 'Hell' to mean separation from Him, the belief in either is a mischievous superstition; for then we have, on the one hand, a merely 'compensatory' belief (a 'sequel' to life's sad story, in which everything will 'come all right') and, on the other, a nightmare which drives men into asylums or makes them persecutors.

Fortunately, by God's good providence, a strong and steady belief of that self-seeking and sub-religious kind is extremely difficult to maintain, and is perhaps possible only to those who are slightly neurotic. Most of us find that our belief in the future life is strong only when God is in the centre of our thoughts; that if we try to use the hope of 'Heaven' as a compensation (even for the most innocent and natural misery, that of bereavement) it crumbles away. It can, on those terms, be maintained only by arduous efforts of controlled imagination; and we know in our hearts that the imagination is our own. As for Hell, I have often been struck, in reading the 'hell-fire sermons' of our older divines, at the desperate efforts they make to render these horrors vivid to their hearers, at their astonishment that men, with such horrors hanging over them, can live as carelessly as they do. But perhaps it is not really astonishing. Perhaps the divines are appealing, on the level of self-centred prudence and self-centred terror, to a belief which, on that level, cannot really exist as a permanent influence on conduct—though of course it may be worked up for a few excited minutes or even hours.

REFLECTIONS ON THE PSALMS

"Death in the Psalms"

Encountering Philosophies of Death

Scripture Readings
Colossians 2:2–6
Psalm 140:1–8

God's will is determined by His wisdom which always perceives, and His goodness which always embraces, the intrinsically good. But when we have said that God commands things only because they are good, we must add that one of the things intrinsically good is that rational creatures should freely surrender themselves to their Creator in obedience. The content of our obedience—the thing we are commanded to do—will always be something intrinsically good, something we ought to do even if (by an impossible supposition) God had not commanded it. But in addition to the content, the mere obeying is also intrinsically good, for, in obeying, a rational creature consciously enacts its creaturely *rôle*, reverses the act by which we fell, treads Adam's dance backward, and returns.

We therefore agree with Aristotle that what is intrinsically right may well be agreeable, and that the better a man is the more he will like it; but we agree with Kant so far as to say that there is one right act—that of self-surrender—which cannot be willed to the height by fallen creatures unless it is unpleasant. And we must add that this one right act includes all other righteousness, and that the supreme cancelling of Adam's fall, the movement 'full speed astern' by which we retrace our long journey from Paradise, the untying of the old, hard knot, must be when the creature, with no desire to aid it, stripped naked to the bare willing of obedience, embraces what is contrary to its nature, and does that for which only one motive is possible. Such an act may be described as a 'test' of the creature's return to God: hence our fathers said that troubles were 'sent to try us'. A familiar example is Abraham's 'trial' when he was ordered to sacrifice Isaac. With the historicity or the morality of that story I am not now concerned, but with the obvious question, 'If God is omniscient He must have known what Abraham would do, without any experiment; why, then, this needless torture?' But as St Augustine points out, whatever God knew, Abraham at any rate did not know that his obedience could endure such a command until the event taught him: and the obedience which he did not know that he would choose, he cannot be said to have chosen. The reality of Abraham's obedience was the act itself; and what God knew in knowing that Abraham 'would obey' was Abraham's actual obedience on that mountain top at that moment. To say that God 'need not have tried the experiment' is to say that because God knows, the thing known by God need not exist.

If pain sometimes shatters the creature's false self-sufficiency, yet in supreme 'Trial' or 'Sacrifice' it teaches him the self-sufficiency which really ought to be his— the 'strength, which, if Heaven gave it, may be called his own': for then, in the absence of all merely natural motives and supports, he acts in that strength, and that alone, which God confers upon him through his subjected will. Human will becomes truly creative and truly our own when it is wholly God's, and this is one of the many senses in which he that loses his soul shall find it. In all other acts our will is fed through nature, that is, through created things other than the self—through the desires which our physical organism and our heredity supply to us. When we act from ourselves alone— that is, from God *in* ourselves—we are collaborators in, or live instruments of, creation: and that is why such an act undoes with 'backward mutters of dissevering power' the uncreative spell which Adam laid upon his species. Hence as suicide is the typical expression of the stoic spirit, and battle of the warrior spirit, martyrdom always remains the supreme enacting and perfection of Christianity. This great action has been initiated for us, done on our behalf, exemplified for our imitation, and inconceivably communicated to all believers, by Christ on Calvary. There the degree of accepted Death reaches the utmost bounds of the imaginable and perhaps goes beyond them; not only all natural supports, but the presence of the very Father to whom the sacrifice is made deserts the victim, and surrender to God does not falter though God 'forsakes' it.

THE PROBLEM OF PAIN

"Human Pain"

Where Is God?

Scripture Readings
Matthew 11:25–30
Psalm 68:17–21

Lewis married later in life, and a few short years after their marriage, Joy died. A Grief Observed *is about that painful time.*

And no one ever told me about the laziness of grief. Except at my job—where the machine seems to run on much as usual—I loathe the slightest effort. Not only writing but even reading a letter is too much. Even shaving. What does it matter now whether my cheek is rough or smooth? They say an unhappy man wants distractions—something to take him out of himself. Only as a dog-tired man wants an extra blanket on a cold night; he'd rather lie there shivering than get up and find one. It's easy to see why the lonely become untidy, finally, dirty and disgusting.

Meanwhile, where is God? This is one of the most disquieting symptoms. When you are happy, so happy that you have no sense of needing Him, so happy that you are tempted to feel His claims upon you as an interruption, if you remember yourself and turn to Him with gratitude and praise, you will be—or so it feels—welcomed with open arms. But go to Him when your need is desperate, when all other help is vain, and what do you find? A door slammed in your face, and a sound of bolting and double bolting on the inside. After that, silence. You may as well turn away. The longer you wait, the more emphatic the silence will become. There are no lights in the windows. It might be an empty house. Was it ever inhabited? It seemed so once. And that seeming was as strong as this. What can this mean? Why is He so present a commander in our time of prosperity and so very absent a help in time of trouble?

I tried to put some of these thoughts to C. this afternoon. He reminded me that the same thing seems to have happened to Christ: 'Why hast thou forsaken me?' I know. Does that make it easier to understand?

Not that I am (I think) in much danger of ceasing to believe in God. The real danger is of coming to believe such dreadful things about Him. The conclusion I dread is not 'So there's no God after all,' but 'So this is what God's really like. Deceive yourself no longer.'

Our elders submitted and said, 'Thy will be done.' How often had bitter resentment been stifled through sheer terror and an act of love—yes, in every sense, an act—put on to hide the operation?

A GRIEF OBSERVED

Chapter 1

WEEK FIVE

New Ways of Recognizing Everyday Glory

Scripture Readings
Matthew 13:18–26
Psalm 25:1–7

Perhaps it seems rather crude to describe glory as the fact of being 'noticed' by God. But this is almost the language of the New Testament. St Paul promises to those who love God not, as we should expect, that they will know Him, but that they will be known by Him (1 Cor. 8:3). It is a strange promise. Does not God know all things at all times? But it is dreadfully re-echoed in another passage of the New Testament. There we are warned that it may happen to anyone of us to appear at last before the face of God and hear only the appalling words, 'I never knew you. Depart from Me.' In some sense, as dark to the intellect as it is unendurable to the feelings, we can be both banished from the presence of Him who is present everywhere and erased from the knowledge of Him who knows all. We can be left utterly and absolutely *outside*—repelled, exiled, estranged, finally and unspeakably ignored. On the other hand, we can be called in, welcomed, received, acknowledged. We walk every day on the razor edge between these two incredible possibilities. Apparently, then, our lifelong nostalgia, our longing to be reunited with something in the universe from which we now feel cut off, to be on the inside of some door which we have always seen from the outside, is no mere neurotic fancy, but the truest index of our real situation. And to be at last summoned inside would be both glory and honour beyond all our merits and also the healing of that old ache.

And this brings me to the other sense of glory—glory as brightness, splendour, luminosity. We are to shine as the sun, we are to be given the Morning Star. I think I begin to see what it means. In one way, of course, God has given us the Morning Star already: you can go and enjoy the gift on many fine mornings if you get up early enough. What more, you may ask, do we want? Ah, but we want so much more—something the books on aesthetics take little notice of. But the poets and the mythologies know all about it. We do not want merely to *see* beauty, though, God knows, even that is bounty enough. We want something else which can hardly be put into words—to be united with the beauty we see, to pass into it, to receive it into ourselves, to bathe in it, to become part of it. That is why we have peopled air and earth and water with gods and goddesses and nymphs and elves—that, though we cannot, yet these projections can enjoy in themselves that beauty, grace, and power of which Nature is the image. That is why the poets tell us such lovely falsehoods. They talk as if the west wind could really sweep into a human soul; but it can't. They tell us that 'beauty born of murmuring sound' will pass into a human face; but it won't. Or not yet. For if we take the imagery of Scripture seriously, if we believe that God will one day give us the Morning Star and cause us to *put on* the splendour of the sun, then we may surmise that both the ancient myths and the modern poetry, so false as history, may be very near the truth as prophecy. At present we are on the outside of the world, the wrong side of the door. We discern the freshness and purity of morning, but they do not make us fresh and pure. We cannot mingle with the splendours we see. But all the leaves of the New Testament are rustling with the rumour that it will not always be so. Some day, God willing, we shall get *in*. When human souls have become as perfect in voluntary obedience as the inanimate creation is in its lifeless obedience, then they will put on its glory, or rather that greater glory of which Nature is only the first sketch. For you must not think that I am putting forward any heathen fancy of being absorbed into Nature. Nature is mortal; we shall outlive her. When all the

113

suns and nebulae have passed away, each one of you will still be alive. Nature is only the image, the symbol; but it is the symbol Scripture invites me to use. We are summoned to pass in through Nature, beyond her, into that splendour which she fitfully reflects.

And in there, in beyond Nature, we shall eat of the tree of life. At present, if we are reborn in Christ, the spirit in us lives directly on God; but the mind and, still more, the body receives life from Him at a thousand removes— through our ancestors, through our food, through the elements. The faint, far-off results of those energies which God's creative rapture implanted in matter when He made the worlds are what we now call physical pleasures; and even thus filtered, they are too much for our present management. What would it be to taste at the fountainhead that stream of which even these lower reaches prove so intoxicating? Yet that, I believe, is what lies before us. The whole man is to drink joy from the fountain of joy. As St Augustine said, the rapture of the saved soul will 'flow over' into the glorified body. In the light of our present specialised and depraved appetites, we cannot imagine this *torrens voluptatis*, and I warn everyone most seriously not to try. But it must be mentioned, to drive out thoughts even more misleading—thoughts that what is saved is a mere ghost, or that the risen body lives in numb insensibility. The body was made for the Lord, and these dismal fancies are wide of the mark.

Meanwhile the cross comes before the crown and to-morrow is a Monday morning. A cleft has opened in the pitiless walls of the world, and we are invited to follow our great Captain inside. The following Him is, of course, the essential point. That being so, it may be asked what practical use there is in the speculations which I have been indulging. I can think of at least one such use. It may be possible for each to think too much of his own potential glory hereafter; it is hardly possible for him to think too often or too deeply about that of his neigh-bour. The load, or weight, or burden of my neighbour's glory should be laid on my back, a load so heavy that only humility can carry it, and the backs of the proud will be broken. It is a serious thing to live in a society of possible gods and goddesses, to remember that the dullest and most uninteresting person you can talk to may one day be a creature which, if you saw it now, you would be strongly tempted to worship, or else a horror and a corruption such as you now meet, if at all, only in a nightmare. All day long we are, in some degree, help-ing each other to one or other of these destinations. It is in the light of these overwhelming possibilities, it is with the awe and the circumspection proper to them, that we should conduct all our dealings with one another, all friendships, all loves, all play, all politics. There are no *ordinary* people. You have never talked to a mere mor-tal. Nations, cultures, arts, civilisations—these are mortal, and their life is to ours as the life of a gnat. But it is immortals whom we joke with, work with, marry, snub, and exploit—immortal horrors or everlasting splendours. This does not mean that we are to be perpetually solemn. We must play. But our merriment must be of that kind (and it is, in fact, the merriest kind) which exists between people who have, from the outset, taken each other seriously—no flippancy, no superiority, no presumption. And our charity must be a real and costly love, with deep feeling for the sins in spite of which we love the sinner—no mere tolerance, or indulgence which parodies love as flippancy parodies merriment. Next to the Blessed Sacrament itself, your neighbour is the holiest object presented to your senses. If he is your Christian neighbour, he is holy in almost the same way, for in him also Christ *vere latitat*—the glorifier and the glorified, Glory Himself, is truly hidden.

THE WEIGHT OF GLORY
"The Weight of Glory"

On a Bus to Heaven

Scripture Readings
Romans 8:14–25
Psalm 25:1–7

The Great Divorce *is a story about people in a bus traveling from Hell to Heaven. This conversation occurs in Heaven.*

'The demand of the loveless and the self-imprisoned that they should be allowed to blackmail the universe: that till they consent to be happy (on their own terms) no one else shall taste joy: that theirs should be the final power; that Hell should be able to *veto* Heaven.'

'I don't know what I want, Sir.'

'Son, son, it must be one way or the other. Either the day must come when joy prevails and all the makers of misery are no longer able to infect it: or else forever and ever the makers of misery can destroy in others the happiness they reject for themselves. I know it has a grand sound to say ye'll accept no salvation which leaves even one creature in the dark outside. But watch that sophistry or ye'll make a Dog in a Manger the tyrant of the universe.'

'But dare one say—it is horrible to say—that Pity must ever die?'

'Ye must distinguish. The action of Pity will live forever: but the passion of Pity will not. The passion of Pity, the Pity we merely suffer, the ache that draws men to concede what should not be conceded and to flatter when they should speak truth, the pity that has cheated many a woman out of her virginity and many a statesman out of his honesty—that will die. It was used as a weapon by bad men against good ones: their weapon will be broken.'

'And what is the other kind—the action?'

'It's a weapon on the other side. It leaps quicker than light from the highest place to the lowest to bring healing and joy, whatever the cost to itself. It changes darkness into light and evil into good. But it will not, at the cunning tears of Hell, impose on good the tyranny of evil. Every disease that submits to a cure shall be cured: but we will not call blue yellow to please those who insist on still having jaundice, nor make a midden of the world's garden for the sake of some who cannot abide the smell of roses.'

'You say it will go down to the lowest, Sir. But she didn't go down with him to Hell. She didn't even see him off by the bus.'

'Where would ye have had her go?'

'Why, where we all came from by that bus. The big gulf, beyond the edge of the cliff. Over there. You can't see it from here, but you must know the place I mean.'

My Teacher gave a curious smile. 'Look,' he said, and with the word he went down on his hands and knees. I did the same (how it hurt my knees!) and presently saw that he had plucked a blade of grass. Using its thin end as a pointer, he made me see, after I had looked very closely, a crack in the soil so small that I could not have identified it without this aid.

'I cannot be certain,' he said, 'that this *is* the crack ye came up through. But through a crack no bigger than that ye certainly came.'

'But—but,' I gasped with a feeling of bewilderment not unlike terror. 'I saw an infinite abyss. And cliffs towering up and up. And then *this* country on top of the cliffs.'

'Aye. But the voyage was not mere locomotion. That bus, and all you inside it, were increasing *in size*.'

'Do you mean then that Hell—all that infinite empty town—is down in some little crack like this?'

'Yes. All Hell is smaller than one pebble of your earthly world: but it is smaller than one atom of *this* world, the Real World. Look at yon butterfly. If it swallowed all Hell, Hell would not be big enough to do it any harm or to have any taste.'

'It seems big enough when you're in it, Sir.'

'And yet all loneliness, angers, hatreds, envies and itchings that it contains, if rolled into one single experience and put into the scale against the least moment of the joy that is felt by the least in Heaven, would have no weight that could be registered at all. Bad cannot succeed even in being bad as truly as good is good. If all Hell's miseries together entered the consciousness of yon wee yellow bird on the bough there, they would be swallowed up without trace, as if one drop of ink had been dropped into that Great Ocean to which your terrestrial Pacific itself is only a molecule.'

'I see,' said I at last. 'She couldn't *fit* into Hell.'

He nodded. 'There's not room for her,' he said. 'Hell could not open its mouth wide enough.'

'And she couldn't make herself smaller?—like Alice, you know.'

'Nothing like small enough. For a damned soul is nearly nothing: it is shrunk, shut up in itself. Good beats upon the damned incessantly as sound waves beat on the ears of the deaf, but they cannot receive it. Their fists are clenched, their teeth are clenched, their eyes fast shut. First they will not, in the end they cannot, open their hands for gifts, or their mouth for food, or their eyes to see.'

'Then no one can ever reach them?'

'Only the Greatest of all can make Himself small

enough to enter Hell. For the higher a thing is, the lower it can descend—a man can sympathise with a horse but a horse cannot sympathise with a rat. Only One has descended into Hell.'

'And will He ever do so again?'

'It was not once long ago that He did it. Time does not work that way when once ye have left the Earth. All moments that have been or shall be were, or are, present in the moment of His descending. There is no spirit in prison to Whom He did not preach.'

THE GREAT DIVORCE

Chapter 13

On the Mystery of Death

Scripture Readings
Hebrews 13:11–16
Psalm 116:1–7

Christ shed tears at the grave of Lazarus and sweated blood in Gethsemane: the Life of Lives that was in Him detested this penal obscenity not less than we do, but more. On the other hand, only he who loses his life will save it. We are baptised into the *death* of Christ, and it is the remedy for the Fall. Death is, in fact, what some modern people call 'ambivalent'. It is Satan's great weapon and also God's great weapon: it is holy and unholy; our supreme disgrace and our only hope; the thing Christ came to conquer and the means by which He conquered.

To penetrate the whole of this mystery is, of course, far beyond our power. If the pattern of Descent and Reascent is (as looks not unlikely) the very formula of reality, then in the mystery of Death the secret of secrets lies hid. But something must be said in order to put the Grand Miracle in its proper light. We need not discuss Death on the highest level of all: the mystical slaying of the Lamb 'before the foundation of the world' is above our speculations. Nor need we consider Death on the lowest level. The death of organisms which are nothing more than organisms, which have developed no personality, does not concern us. Of it we may truly say, as some spiritually minded people would have us say of human Death, that it 'doesn't matter'. But the startling Christian doctrine of human Death cannot be passed over.

Human Death, according to the Christians, is a result of human sin; Man, as originally created, was immune from it: Man, when redeemed, and recalled to a new life (which will, in some undefined sense, be a bodily life) in the midst of a more organic and more fully obedient Nature, will be immune from it again. This doctrine is of course simply nonsense if a man is nothing but a Natural organism. But if he were, then, as we have seen, all thoughts would be equally nonsensical, for all would have irrational causes. Man must therefore be a composite being—a natural organism tenanted by, or in a state of *symbiosis* with, a supernatural spirit. The Christian doctrine, startling as it must seem to those who have not fully cleared their minds of Naturalism, states that the relations which we now observe between that spirit and that organism, are abnormal or pathological ones. At present spirit can retain its foothold against the incessant counter-attacks of Nature (both physiological and psychological) only by perpetual vigilance, and physiological Nature always defeats it in the end. Sooner or later it becomes unable to resist the disintegrating processes at work in the body and death ensues. A little later the Natural organism (for it does not long enjoy its triumph) is similarly conquered by merely physical Nature and returns to the inorganic. But, on the Christian view, this was not always so. The spirit was once not a garrison, maintaining its post with difficulty in a hostile Nature, but was fully 'at home' with its organism, like a king in his own country or a rider on his own horse—or better still, as the human part of a Centaur was 'at home' with the equine part. Where spirit's power over the organism was complete and unresisted, death would never occur. No doubt, spirit's permanent triumph over natural forces which, if left to themselves, would kill the organism, would involve a continued miracle: but only the same sort of miracle which occurs every day—for whenever we think rationally we are, by direct spiritual power, forcing certain atoms in our brain and certain psychological tendencies in our natural soul to do what they would never have done if left to Nature. The Christian doctrine would be fantastic only if the present frontier-situation between spirit and Nature in each human being were so intelligible and self-explanatory that we just 'saw' it to be the only one that could ever have existed.

MIRACLES

"The Grand Miracle"

Sonnets on Heaven

Scripture Readings
Revelation 3:19–22
Psalm 78:23–39

1.

You think that we who do not shout and shake
Our fists at God when youth or bravery die
Have colder blood or hearts less apt to ache
Than yours who rail. I know you do. Yet why?
You have what sorrow always long to find,
Someone to blame, some enemy in chief;
Anger's the anaesthetic of the mind,
It does men good, it fumes away their grief.
We feel the stroke like you; so far our fate
Is equal. After that, for us begin
Half-hopeless labours, learning not to hate,
And then to want, and then (perhaps) to win
A high, unearthly comfort, angel's food,
That seems at first mockery to flesh and blood.

2.

There's a repose, a safety (even a taste
Of something like revenge?) in fixed despair
Which we're forbidden. We have to rise with haste
And start to climb what seems a crazy stair.
Our consolation (for we are consoled,
So much of us, I mean, as may be left
After the dreadful process has unrolled)
For one bereavement makes us more bereft.
It asks for all we have, to the last shred;
Read Dante, who had known its best and worst—
He was bereaved and he was comforted
—No one denies it, comforted—but first
Down to the frozen centre, up the vast
Mountain of pain, from world to world, he passed.

3.

Of this we're certain; no one who dared knock
At heaven's door for earthly comfort found
Even a door—only smooth, endless rock,
And save the echo of his cry no sound.
It's dangerous to listen; you'll begin
To fancy that those echoes (hope can play
Pitiful tricks) are answers from within;
Far better to turn, grimly sane, away.
Heaven cannot thus, Earth cannot ever, give
The thing we want. We ask what isn't there

And by our asking water and make live
That very part of love which must despair
And die and go down cold into the earth
Before there's talk of springtime and re-birth.

4.

Pitch your demands heaven-high and they'll be met.
Ask for the Morning Star and take (thrown in)
Your earthly love. Why, yes; but how to set
One's foot on the first rung, how to begin?
The silence of one voice upon our ears
Beats like the waves; the coloured morning seems
A lying brag; the face we loved appears
Fainter each night, or ghastlier, in our dreams.
'That long way round which Dante trod was meant
For mighty saints and mystics not for me,'
So Nature cries. Yet if we once assent
To Nature's voice, we shall be like the bee
That booms against the window-pane for hours
Thinking that way to reach the laden flowers.

5.

'If we could speak to her,' my doctor said,
'And told her, "Not that way! All, all in vain
You weary out your wings and bruise your head,"
Might she not answer, buzzing at the pane,
"Let queens and mystics and religious bees

Talk of such inconceivables as glass;
The blunt lay worker flies at what she sees,
Look there—ahead, ahead—the flowers, the grass!"
We catch her in a handkerchief (who knows
What rage she feels, what terror, what despair?)
And shake her out—and gaily out she goes
Where quivering flowers stand thick in summer air,
To drink their hearts. But left to her own will
She would have died upon the window-sill.'

POEMS
'Five Sonnets'

Encountering Aslan

Scripture Readings
II Corinthians 5:14–21
Psalm 40:1–5

Next moment the whole world seemed to turn upside down, and the children felt as if they had left their insides behind them; for the Lion had gathered himself together for a greater leap than any he had yet made and jumped—or you may call it flying rather than jumping—right over the castle wall. The two girls, breathless but unhurt, found themselves tumbling off his back in the middle of a wide stone courtyard full of statues.

'What an extraordinary place!' cried Lucy. 'All those stone animals—and people too! It's—it's like a museum.'

'Hush,' said Susan, 'Aslan's doing something.'

He was indeed. He had bounded up to the stone lion and breathed on him. Then without waiting a moment he whisked round—almost as if he had been a cat chasing its tail—and breathed also on the stone dwarf, which (as you remember) was standing a few feet from the lion with his back to it. Then he pounced on a tall stone Dryad which stood beyond the dwarf, turned rapidly aside to deal with a stone rabbit on his right, and rushed on to two centaurs. But at that moment Lucy said,

'Oh, Susan! Look! Look at the lion.'

I expect you've seen someone put a lighted match to a bit of newspaper which is propped up in a grate against an unlit fire. And for a second nothing seems to have happened; and then you notice a tiny streak of flame creeping along the edge of the newspaper. It was like that now. For a second after Aslan had breathed upon him the stone lion looked just the same. Then a tiny streak of gold began to run along his white marble back—then it spread—then the colour seemed to lick all over him as the flame licks all over a bit of paper—then, while his hind-quarters were still obviously stone the lion shook his mane and all the heavy, stony folds rippled into living hair. Then he opened a great red mouth, warm and living, and gave a prodigious yawn. And now his hind legs had come to life. He lifted one of them and scratched himself. Then, having caught sight of Aslan, he went bounding after him and frisking round him whimpering with delight and jumping up to lick his face.

Of course the children's eyes turned to follow the lion; but the sight they saw was so wonderful that they soon forgot about *him*. Everywhere the statues were coming to life. The courtyard looked no longer like a museum; it looked more like a zoo. Creatures were running after Aslan and dancing round him till he was almost hidden in the crowd. Instead of all that deadly white the courtyard was now a blaze of colours; glossy chestnut sides of centaurs, indigo horns of unicorns, dazzling plumage of birds, reddy-brown of foxes, dogs, and satyrs, yellow stockings and crimson hoods of dwarfs; and the birch-girls in silver, and the beech-girls in fresh, transparent green, and the larch-girls in green so bright that it was almost yellow. And instead of the deadly silence the whole place rang with the sound of happy roarings, brayings, yelpings, barkings, squealings, cooings, neighings, stampings, shouts, hurrahs, songs and laughter.

'Ooh!' said Susan in a different tone. 'Look! I wonder— I mean, is it safe?'

Lucy looked and saw that Aslan had just breathed on the feet of the stone giant.

'It's all right!' shouted Aslan joyously. 'Once the feet are put right, all the rest of him will follow.'

THE LION, THE WITCH AND THE WARDROBE
"What Happened with the Statues"

Launcelot

Scripture Readings
Hebrews 9:11–15
Psalm 23:1–6

"Launcelot" is a long narrative poem about chivalry and the pilgrimaging spirit. Lewis likely wrote this before his conversion sometime in the early 1930s, yet faith is still at the story's center.

'Listen: there are two sorts of the unseen,
Two countries each from each removed as far
As the black dungeons of this castle are
From this green mountain and this golden sun.
And of the first, I say, we do not know;
But the other is beneath, where to and fro
Through echoing vaults continually chaos vast
Works in the cellarage of the soul, and things exiled,
And foolish giants howling from the ancestral past
Wander, and overweening Hopes, and Fears too wild

For this slow-ripening universe; chimeras, ghosts,
And succubi and cruelties. You are more like,
Driven on by such a fury of desire, to strike
Those rocks than to make harbour on the happy
    coasts.
Wishing is perilous work.'

                        'Go on,' she said.
'What more?' the Bishop asked, and turned his head
Slowly away; 'What more is there to tell?'
'You have described the downward journey well,
But of the realm of light, have you no word?'

'Nothing but that which all mankind have heard.'

She turned away, she paced the floor,
She waited for the Bishop's word no more.
And he looked down, and more than once he passed
His hand across his face, and then at last
Spoke gently, as a man in much distress.
'Daughter,' he said, 'I see I must confess.
God knows I am an old, fat, sleek divine
—Lived easily all my life—far deeper skilled
In nice discriminations of old wine
Than in those things for which God's blood was
    spilled.
Enough of that. And now my punishment
Has found me and my time of grace is spent;

For now I must speak truth and find at need
My advocacy kills the cause I plead.
For if I say none knows, no man is sure
Of anything about that land, your eyes,
Seeing me thus world-ridden, thus impure,
How can they, if they would, judge otherwise
Than that my disallegiance from the laws
Of Spirit has dulled my edge and been the cause
Of this great ignorance I profess? How, then,
Believe me when I teach that holiest men
Are not less ignorant? (So I think, but I—
What do I know of saints or sanctity?)
But so I think; and so perforce I come
Into the court, though shamed, not daring to be
    dumb.
Hear, then, my tale.
I, who stand ignorant confessed,
Doctor of nescience, or, at best,
A plodding passman in the school
Meek Wonder and her maidens rule,
Who hold the brave world's blue and green
But for a magic-lantern screen
That enigmatically shows
The shadow of what no one knows;—
I yet believe (if such a word
Of these soiled lips be not absurd)
That from the place beyond all ken

One only Word has come to men,
And was incarnate and had hands
And feet and walked in earthly lands
And died, and rose. And nothing more
Will come or ever came before
With certainty. And to obey
Is better than the hard assay
Of piercing anywhere besides
This mortal veil, which haply hides
Some insupportable abyss
Of bodiless light and burning bliss.
Hence, if you ask me of the way
Yonder, what can I do but say
Over again (as God's own Son
Seems principally to have done)
The lessons of your nurse and mother?
For all my counsel is no other
Than this, now given at bitterest need;
—Go, learn your catechism and creed.
Mark what I say, not how I live,
And for myself—may God forgive.'

'I thought as much,' she cried. 'That pale,
Numbing, inevitable tale,
The deathbed of desire! Why do you cease?
Preach out your sermon, tell me now of peace
Of passions calmed with grey renunciation,

Longsuffering and obedience and salvation!
What is all this to me? Where is my home
Save where the immortals in their exultation,
Moon-led, their holy hills forever roam?
What is to me your sanctity, grave-clothed in white,
Cold as an altar, pale as altar candle light?
Not to such purpose was the plucking at my heart
Wherever beauty called me into lonely places,
Where dark Remembrance haunts me with eternal
      smart,
Remembrance, the unmerciful, the well of love,
Recalling the far dances, the far-distant faces,
Whispering me "What does this—and this—remind
      you of?"
How can I cease from knocking or forget to watch—'

NARRATIVE POEMS

"Launcelot"

Aging: A Partial Awakening

Scripture Readings
Isaiah 55:1–7
Psalm 37:23–26

Lewis's letters sometimes provide a raw glimpse into his daily feelings. This is one of a number of letters to Warfield M. Firor of Baltimore, Maryland, a surgeon at Johns Hopkins.

Today the less pleasant side of Autumn has showed itself for the first time. Up till now it has been paradisal, the sort of weather which for some reason excites me much more than spring: cool, cobwebby mornings developing into the mildest sunlight, and exquisite colours in the woods. It always gives me *Wanderlust* & 'divine discontent' and all that. Today we have had a low, dirty, smoke-coloured sky racing overhead and a steady down-pour. That, however, has no causal connection (chronology proves it) with the subject that is uppermost in my mind and has been for some days: Old Age.

You are a bit further on the road than I am and will probably smile at a man whose fifty-first birthday is still several weeks ahead starting his meditation *de senectute*. Yet why? The realisation must *begin* sometime. In one way, of course (no, in two) it began much earlier. (1) With the growing realisation that there were a great many things one wd. never have time to do. Those golden days when one could still think it possible that one might some time take up a quite new study: say Persian, or Geology, were now definitely over. (2) Harder to express. I mean, the end of that period when every goal, besides being itself, was an earnest or promise of much more to come. Like a pretty girl at her first dance: valued not chiefly for itself but as the prelude to a whole new world. Do you remember the time when every pleasure (say, the smell of a hayfield or a country walk, or a swim) was big with futurity and bore on its face the notice 'Lots more where I came from'? Well, there's a change from that to the period when they all begin to say 'Make the most of me: my predecessors outnumber my successors'.

Both these two feelings—the twitch of the tether and the loss of promise—I have had for a long time. What has come lately is much harsher—the arctic wind of the future catching one, so to speak, at a corner. The particular corner was the sharp realisation that I shall be compulsorily 'retired' in 1959, and the infernal *nuisance* (to put it no higher) of patching up some new sort of life somewhere.

You will not suppose I am putting these things as lamentations: that, to a man older than oneself, wd. be very odd. They are merely the *data*. (Add, of course, among them, the probable loss of friends, especially if, like me, one has the imprudent habit of making more friends among one's seniors than among one's juniors.) And as usual, the result of all this (wd. you agree?) is almost entirely good.

Have you ever thought what it wd. be like if (all other things remaining as they are) old age and death had been made optional? *All other things remaining*: i.e., it wd. still be true that our real destiny was elsewhere, that we have no abiding city here and no true happiness, *but* the un-hitching from this life was left to be accomplished by our own will as an act of obedience & faith. I suppose the percentage of *diers* wd. be about the same as the percentage of Trappists is now.

I am therefore (with some help from the weather and rheumatism!) trying to profit by this new realisation of my mortality. To begin to die, to loosen a few of the tentacles which the octopus-world has fastened on one. But of course it is continuings, not beginnings, that are the point. A good night's sleep, a sunny morning, a success with my next book—any of these will, I know, alter the whole thing. Which alteration, by the bye, being in reality a relapse from partial waking into the old stupor, wd. nevertheless be regarded by most people as a returning to health from a 'morbid' mood!

Well, it's certainly not that. But it is a *very* partial waking. One ought not to need the gloomy moments of life for beginning detachment, nor be re-entangled by the bright ones. One ought to be able to enjoy the bright ones to the full and at that very moment have the perfect readiness to leave them, confident that what calls one away is better. . . .

LETTERS OF C. S. LEWIS
15 October 1949

WEEK SIX

The Purpose of Pain

Scripture Readings
Revelation 21:1–8
Psalm 40:1–5

The doctrine of death which I describe is not peculiar to Christianity. Nature herself has written it large across the world in the repeated drama of the buried seed and the re-arising corn. From nature, perhaps, the oldest agricultural communities learned it and with animal, or human, sacrifices showed forth for centuries the truth that 'without shedding of blood is no remission'; and though at first such conceptions may have concerned only the crops and offspring of the tribe, they came later, in the Mysteries, to concern the spiritual death and resurrection of the individual. The Indian ascetic, mortifying his body on a bed of spikes, preaches the same lesson; the Greek philosopher tells us that the life of wisdom is 'a practise of death'. The sensitive and noble heathen of modern times makes his imagined gods 'die into life'. Mr

Huxley expounds 'non-attachment'. We cannot escape the doctrine by ceasing to be Christians. It is an 'eternal gospel' revealed to men wherever men have sought, or endured, the truth: it is the very nerve of redemption, which anatomising wisdom at all times and in all places lays bare; the unescapable knowledge which the Light that lighteneth every man presses down upon the minds of all who seriously question what the universe is 'about'. The peculiarity of the Christian faith is not to teach this doctrine but to render it, in various ways, more tolerable. Christianity teaches us that the terrible task has already in some sense been accomplished for us—that a master's hand is holding ours as we attempt to trace the difficult letters and that our script need only be a 'copy', not an original. Again, where other systems expose our total nature to death (as in Buddhist renunciation) Christianity demands only that we set right a *misdirection* of our nature, and has no quarrel, like Plato, with the body as such, nor with the psychical elements in our make-up. And sacrifice in its supreme realisation is not exacted of all. Confessors as well as martyrs are saved, and some old people whose state of grace we can hardly doubt seem to have got through their seventy years surprisingly easily. The sacrifice of Christ is repeated, or re-echoed, among His followers in very varying degrees, from the cruellest martyrdom down to a self-submission of intention whose outward signs have nothing to distinguish them from the ordinary fruits of temperance and 'sweet reasonableness'. The causes of this distribution I do not know; but from our present point of view it ought to be clear that the real problem is not why some humble, pious, believing people suffer, but why some do *not*. Our Lord Himself, it will be remembered, explained the salvation of those who are fortunate in this world only by referring to the unsearchable omnipotence of God.

All arguments in justification of suffering provoke bitter resentment against the author. You would like to know how I behave when I am experiencing pain, not writing books about it. You need not guess, for I will tell you; I am a great coward. But what is that to the purpose? When I think of pain—of anxiety that gnaws like fire and loneliness that spreads out like a desert, and the heartbreaking routine of monotonous misery, or again of dull aches that blacken our whole landscape or sudden nauseating pains that knock a man's heart out at one blow, of pains that seem already intolerable and then are suddenly increased, of infuriating scorpion-stinging pains that startle into maniacal movement a man who seemed half dead with his previous tortures—it 'quite o'ercrows my spirit'. If I knew any way of escape I would crawl through sewers to find it. But what is the good of telling you about my feelings? You know them already: they are the same as yours. I am not arguing that pain is not painful. Pain hurts. That is what the word means. I am only trying to show that the old Christian doctrine of being made 'perfect through suffering' is not incredible. To prove it palatable is beyond my design.

In estimating the credibility of the doctrine two principles ought to be observed. In the first place we must remember that the actual moment of present pain is only the centre of what may be called the whole tribulational system which extends itself by fear and pity. Whatever good effects these experiences have are dependent upon the centre; so that even if pain itself was of no spiritual value, yet, if fear and pity were, pain would have to exist in order that there should be something to be feared and pitied. And that fear and pity help us in our return to obedience and charity is not to be doubted. Everyone has experienced the effect of pity in making it easier for us to love the unlovely—that is, to love men not because they are in any way naturally agreeable to us but because they are our brethren. The beneficence of fear most of us have learned during the period of 'crises' that led up to the present war. My own experience is something like this. I am progressing along the path of life in my ordinary contentedly fallen and godless condition, absorbed in a merry meeting with my friends for the morrow or a bit of work that tickles my vanity today, a holiday or a new book, when suddenly a stab of abdominal pain that threatens serious disease, or a headline in the newspapers that threatens us all with destruction, sends this whole pack of cards tumbling down. At first I am overwhelmed, and all my little happinesses look like broken toys. Then, slowly and reluctantly, bit by bit, I try to bring myself into the frame of mind that I should be in at all times. I remind myself that all these toys were never intended to possess my heart, that my true good is in another world and my only real treasure is Christ. And perhaps, by God's grace, I succeed, and for a day or two become a creature consciously dependent on God and drawing its strength from the right sources. But the moment the threat is withdrawn, my whole nature leaps back to the toys: I am even anxious, God forgive me, to banish from my mind the only thing that supported me under the threat because it is now associated with the misery of those few days. Thus the terrible necessity of tribulation is only too clear. God has had me for but forty-eight hours and then only by dint of taking everything else away from me. Let Him but sheathe that sword for a moment and I behave like a puppy when the hated bath is over—I shake myself as dry as I can and race off to reacquire my comfortable dirtiness, if not in the nearest manure heap, at least in the nearest flower bed. And that is why tribulations cannot cease until God either sees us remade or sees that our remaking is now hopeless.

THE PROBLEM OF PAIN
"Human Pain"

Encountering the Spirit

Scripture Readings
Ephesians 4:7–13
Psalm 19:1–6

Surprised by Joy is Lewis's autobiography. The reading for today and tomorrow is Lewis recalling some early moments of God's prodding him toward Christianity, a conversion experience that would happen on an early morning in 1933 with friends J. R. R. Tolkien and Hugo Dyson at his side.

Then I read Chesterton's *Everlasting Man* and for the first time saw the whole Christian outline of history set out in a form that seemed to me to make sense. Somehow I contrived not to be too badly shaken. You will remember that I already thought Chesterton the most sensible man alive 'apart from his Christianity'. Now, I veritably believe, I thought—I didn't of course *say*; words would have revealed the nonsense—that Christianity itself was very sensible 'apart from its Christianity'. But I hardly remember, for I had not long finished *The Everlasting Man* when something far more alarming happened to me. Early in 1926 the hardest boiled of all the atheists I ever knew sat in my room on the other side of the fire and remarked that the evidence for the historicity of the Gospels was really surprisingly good. 'Rum thing,' he went on. 'All that stuff of Frazer's about the Dying God. Rum thing. It almost looks as if it had really happened once.' To understand the shattering impact of it, you would need to know the man (who has certainly never since shown any interest in Christianity). If he, the cynic of cynics, the toughest of toughs, were not—as I would still have put it—'safe', where could I turn? Was there then no escape?

The odd thing was that before God closed in on me, I was in fact offered what now appears a moment of wholly free choice. In a sense. I was going up Headington Hill on the top of a bus. Without words and (I think) almost without images, a fact about myself was somehow presented to me. I became aware that I was holding something at bay, or shutting something out. Or, if you like, that I was wearing some stiff clothing, like corsets, or even a suit of armour, as if I were a lobster. I felt myself being, there and then, given a free choice. I could open the door or keep it shut; I could unbuckle the armour or keep it on. Neither choice was presented as a duty; no threat or promise was attached to either, though I knew that to open the door or to take off the corslet meant the incalculable. The choice appeared to be momentous but it was also strangely unemotional. I was moved by no desires or fears. In a sense I was not moved by anything. I chose to open, to unbuckle, to loosen the rein. I say, 'I chose', yet it did not really seem possible to do the opposite. On the other hand, I was aware of no motives. You could argue that I was not a free agent, but I am more inclined to think that this came nearer to being a perfectly free act than most that I have ever done. Necessity may not be the opposite of freedom, and perhaps a man is most free when, instead of producing motives, he could only say, 'I am what I do.' Then came the repercussion on the imaginative level. I felt as if I were a man of snow at long last beginning to melt. The melting was starting in my back—drip-drip and presently trickle-trickle. I rather disliked the feeling.

The fox had been dislodged from Hegelian Wood and was now running in the open, 'with all the wo in the world', bedraggled and weary, hounds barely a field behind. And nearly everyone now (one way or another) in the pack; Plato, Dante, MacDonald, Herbert, Barfield, Tolkien, Dyson, Joy itself. Everyone and everything had joined the other side. Even my own pupil Griffiths—now Dom Bede Griffiths—though not yet himself a believer, did his share. Once, when he and Barfield were lunching in my room, I happened to refer to philosophy as 'a subject'. 'It wasn't a subject to Plato,' said Barfield, 'it was a way.' The quiet but fervent agreement of Griffiths, and the quick glance of understanding between these two, revealed to me my own frivolity. Enough had been thought, and said, and felt, and imagined. It was about time that something should be done.

For of course there had long been an ethic (theoretically) attached to my Idealism. I thought the business of us finite and half-unreal souls was to multiply the consciousness of Spirit by seeing the world from different positions while yet remaining qualitatively the same as Spirit; to be tied to a particular time and place and set of circumstances, yet there to will and think as Spirit itself does. This was hard; for the very act whereby Spirit projected souls and a world gave those souls different and competitive interests, so that there was a temptation to selfishness. But I thought each of us had it in his power to discount the emotional perspective produced by his own particular selfhood, just as we discount the optical perspective produced by our position in space. To prefer my own happiness to my neighbour's was like thinking that the nearest telegraph post was really the largest. The way to recover, and act upon, this universal and objective vision was daily and hourly to remember our true nature, to reascend or return into that Spirit which, in so far as we really were at all, we still were. Yes: but I now felt I had better try to do it. I faced at last (in Mac-Donald's words) 'something to be neither more nor less nor other than *done*'. An attempt at complete virtue must be made. Really, a young Atheist cannot guard his faith too carefully. Dangers lie in wait for him on every side. You must not do, you must not even try to do, the will of the Father unless you are prepared to 'know of the doctrine'. All my acts, desires, and thoughts were to be brought into harmony with universal Spirit. For the first time I examined myself with a seriously practical purpose. And there I found what appalled me; a zoo of lusts, a bedlam of ambitions, a nursery of fears, a hareem of fondled hatreds.

My name was legion.

Of course I could do nothing—I could not last out one hour—without continual conscious recourse to what I called Spirit. But the fine, philosophical distinction between this and what ordinary people call 'prayer to God' breaks down as soon as you start doing it in earnest.

SURPRISED BY JOY
"Checkmate"

Encountering the Spirit, Part II

Scripture Readings
Isaiah 55:8–13
Psalm 19:7–14

Idealism can be talked, and even felt; it cannot be lived. It became patently absurd to go on thinking of 'Spirit' as either ignorant of, or passive to, my approaches. Even if my own philosophy were true, how could the initiative lie on my side? My own analogy, as I now first perceived, suggested the opposite: if Shakespeare and Hamlet could ever meet, it must be Shakespeare's doing. Hamlet could initiate nothing. Perhaps, even now, my Absolute Spirit still differed in some way from the God of religion. The real issue was not, or not yet, there. The real terror was that if you seriously believed in even such a 'God' or 'Spirit' as I admitted, a wholly new situation developed. As the dry bones shook and came together in that dreadful valley of Ezekiel's, so now a philosophical theorem, cerebrally entertained, began to stir and heave and throw off its gravecloths, and stood upright and became a living presence. I was to be allowed to play at philosophy no longer. It might, as I say, still be true that my 'Spirit' differed in some way from 'the God of popular religion'. My Adversary waived the point. It sank into utter unimportance. He would not argue about it. He only said, 'I am the Lord'; 'I am that I am'; 'I am.'

People who are naturally religious find difficulty in understanding the horror of such a revelation. Amiable agnostics will talk cheerfully about 'man's search for God'. To me, as I then was, they might as well have talked about the mouse's search for the cat. The best image of my predicament is the meeting of Mime and Wotan in the first act of Siegfried; *bier brauch' ich nicht Sparer noch Spiiher, Einsam will ich* . . . (I've no use for spies and snoopers. I would be private . . .).

Remember, I had always wanted, above all things, not to be 'interfered with'. I had wanted (mad wish) 'to call my soul my own'. I had been far more anxious to avoid suffering than to achieve delight. I had always aimed at limited liabilities. The supernatural itself had been to me, first, an illicit dram, and then, as by a drunkard's reaction, nauseous. Even my recent attempt to live my philosophy had secretly (I now knew) been hedged round by all sorts of reservations. I had pretty well known that my ideal of virtue would never be allowed to lead me into anything intolerably painful; I would be 'reasonable'. But now what had been an ideal became a command; and what might not be expected of one? Doubtless, by definition, God was Reason itself. But would He also be 'reasonable' in that other, more comfortable, sense? Not the slightest assurance on that score was offered me. Total surrender, the absolute leap in the dark, were demanded. The reality with which no treaty can be made was upon me. The demand was not even 'All or nothing'. I think that stage had been passed, on the bus-top when I unbuckled my armour and the snow-man started to melt. Now, the demand was simply 'All'.

You must picture me alone in that room at Magdalen, night after night, feeling, whenever my mind lifted even for a second from my work, the steady, unrelenting approach of Him whom I so earnestly desired not to meet. That which I greatly feared had at last come upon me. In the Trinity Term of 1929 I gave in, and admitted that God was God, and knelt and prayed: perhaps, that night, the most dejected and reluctant convert in all England. I did not then see what is now the most shining and obvious thing; the Divine humility which will accept a convert even on such terms. The Prodigal Son at least walked home on his own feet. But who can duly adore that Love which will open the high gates to a prodigal who is brought in kicking, struggling, resentful, and darting his eyes in every direction for a chance of escape? The words *compelle intrare*, compel them to come in, have been so abused by wicked men that we shudder at them; but, properly understood, they plumb the depth of the Divine mercy. The hardness of God is kinder than the softness of men, and His compulsion is our liberation.

SURPRISED BY JOY
"Checkmate"

God, Our Model to Imitate

Scripture Readings
Jude 1:20–24
Psalm 25:8–11

I said that when we see how all our plans shipwreck on the characters of the people we have to deal with, we are 'in *one* way' seeing what it must be like for God. But only in one way. There are two respects in which God's view must be very different from ours. In the first place, He sees (like you) how all the people in your home or your job are in various degrees awkward or difficult; but when He looks into that home or factory or office He sees one more person of the same kind—the one you never do see. I mean, of course, yourself. That is the next great step in wisdom—to realise that you also are just that sort of person. You also have a fatal flaw in your character. All the hopes and plans of others have again and again shipwrecked on your character just as your hopes and plans have shipwrecked on theirs.

It is no good passing this over with some vague, general admission such as 'Of course, I know I have my faults.' It is important to realise that there is some really fatal flaw in you: something which gives the others just that same feeling of despair which their flaws give you. And it is almost certainly something you don't know about—like what the advertisements call 'halitosis', which everyone notices except the person who has it. But why, you ask, don't the others tell me? Believe me, they have tried to tell you over and over again, and you just couldn't 'take it'. Perhaps a good deal of what you call their 'nagging' or 'bad temper' or 'queerness' are just their attempts to make you see the truth. And even the faults you do know you don't know fully. You say, 'I admit I lost my temper last night'; but the others know that you're always doing it, that you are a bad-tempered person. You say, 'I admit I drank too much last Saturday'; but everyone else knows that you are a habitual drunkard.

That is one way in which God's view must differ from mine. He sees all the characters: I see all except my own. But the second difference is this. He loves the people in spite of their faults. He goes on loving. He does not let go. Don't say, 'It's all very well for Him; He hasn't got to live with them.' He has. He is inside them as well as outside them. He is with them far more intimately and closely and incessantly than we can ever be. Every vile thought within their minds (and ours), every moment of spite, envy, arrogance, greed, and self-conceit comes right up against His patient and longing love, and grieves His spirit more than it grieves ours.

The more we can imitate God in both these respects, the more progress we shall make. We must love 'X' more; and we must learn to see ourselves as a person of exactly the same kind. Some people say it is morbid to be always thinking of one's own faults. That would be all very well if most of us could stop thinking of our own without soon beginning to think about those of other people. For unfortunately we *enjoy* thinking about other people's faults: and in the proper sense of the word 'morbid', that is the most morbid pleasure in the world.

GOD IN THE DOCK
"The Trouble with 'X'"

A Conversion Scenario

Scripture Readings
II Peter 2:4–22
Psalm 55:15–19

Let us try to be honest with ourselves. Picture to yourself a man who has risen to wealth or power by a continued course of treachery and cruelty, by exploiting for purely selfish ends the noble motions of his victims, laughing the while at their simplicity; who, having thus attained success, uses it for the gratification of lust and hatred and finally parts with the last rag of honour among thieves by betraying his own accomplices and jeering at their last moments of bewildered disillusionment. Suppose, further, that he does all this, not (as we like to imagine) tormented by remorse or even misgiving, but eating like a schoolboy and sleeping like a healthy infant—a jolly, ruddy-cheeked man, without a care in the world, unshakably confident to the very end that he alone has found the answer to the riddle of life, that God and man are fools whom he has got the better of, that his way of life is utterly successful, satisfactory, unassailable. We must be careful at this point. The least indulgence of the passion for revenge is very deadly sin. Christian charity counsels us to make every effort for the conversion of such a man: to prefer his conversion, at the peril of our own lives, perhaps of our own souls, to his punishment; to prefer it infinitely. But that is not the question. Supposing he *will* not be converted, what destiny in the eternal world can you regard as proper for him? Can you really desire that such a man, *remaining what he is* (and he must be able to do that if he has free will) should be confirmed forever in his present happiness—should continue, for all eternity, to be perfectly convinced that the laugh is on his side? And if you cannot regard this as tolerable, is it only your wickedness—only spite—that prevents you from doing so? Or do you find that conflict between Justice and Mercy, which has sometimes seemed to you such an outmoded piece of theology, now actually at work in your own mind, and feeling very much as if it came to you from above, not from below? You are moved not by a desire for the wretched creature's pain as such, but by a truly ethical demand that, soon or late, the right should be asserted, the flag planted in this horribly rebellious soul, even if no fuller and better conquest is to follow. In a sense, it is better for the creature itself, even if it never becomes good, that it should know itself a failure, a mistake. Even mercy can hardly wish to such a man his eternal, contented continuance in such ghastly illusion. Thomas Aquinas said of suffering, as Aristotle had said of shame, that it was a thing not good in itself; but a thing which might have a certain goodness in particular circumstances. That is to say, if evil is present, pain at recognition of the evil, being a kind of knowledge, is relatively good; for the alternative is that the soul should be ignorant of the evil, or ignorant that the evil is contrary to its nature, 'either of which', says the philosopher, 'is *manifestly* bad'. And I think, though we tremble, we agree.

The demand that God should forgive such a man while he remains what he is, is based on a confusion between condoning and forgiving. To condone an evil is simply to ignore it, to treat it as if it were good. But forgiveness needs to be accepted as well as offered if it is to be complete: and a man who admits no guilt can accept no forgiveness.

I have begun with the conception of Hell as a positive retributive punishment inflicted by God because that is the form in which the doctrine is most repellent, and I wished to tackle the strongest objection. But, of course, though Our Lord often speaks of Hell as a sentence inflicted by a tribunal, He also says elsewhere that the judgement consists in the very fact that men prefer darkness to light, and that not He, but His 'word', judges men. We are therefore at liberty—since the two conceptions, in the long run, mean the same thing—to think of this bad man's perdition not as a sentence imposed on him but as the mere fact of being what he is. The characteristic of lost souls is 'their rejection of everything that is not simply themselves'. Our imaginary egoist has tried to turn everything he meets into a province or appendage of the self. The taste for the *other*, that is, the very capacity for enjoying good, is quenched in him except in so far as his body still draws him into some rudimentary contact with an outer world. Death removes this last contact. He has his wish—to lie wholly in the self and to make the best of what he finds there. And what he finds there is Hell.

THE PROBLEM OF PAIN
"Hell"

In Love, He Claims All

Scripture Readings
Luke 9:21–26
Psalm 86:1–7

This is my endlessly recurrent temptation: to go down to that sea (I think St John of the Cross called God a sea) and there neither dive nor swim nor float, but only dabble and splash, careful not to get out of my depth and holding on to the lifeline which connects me with my things temporal.

It is different from the temptations that met us at the beginning of the Christian life. Then we fought (at least I fought) against admitting the claims of the eternal at all. And when we had fought, and been beaten, and surrendered, we supposed that all would be fairly plain sailing. This temptation comes later. It is addressed to those who have already admitted the claim in principle and are even making some sort of effort to meet it. Our temptation is to look eagerly for the minimum that will be accepted. We are in fact very like honest but reluctant taxpayers. We approve of an income tax in principle. We make our returns truthfully. But we dread a rise in the tax. We are very careful to pay no more than is necessary. And we hope—we very ardently hope—that after we have paid it there will still be enough left to live on.

And notice that those cautions which the tempter whispers in our ears are all plausible. Indeed, I don't think he often tries to deceive us (after early youth) with a direct lie. The plausibility is this. It is really possible to be carried away by religious emotion—*enthusiasm* as our ancestors called it—into resolutions and attitudes which we shall, not sinfully but rationally, not when we are more worldly but when we are wiser, have cause to regret. We can become scrupulous or fanatical; we can, in what seems zeal but is really presumption, embrace tasks never intended for us. That is the truth in the temptation. The lie consists in the suggestion that our best protection is a prudent regard for the safety of our pocket, our habitual indulgences, and our ambitions. But that is quite false. Our real protection is to be sought elsewhere: in common Christian usage, in moral theology, in steady rational thinking, in the advice of good friends and good books, and (if need be) in a skilled spiritual director. Swimming lessons are better than a lifeline to the shore.

For of course that lifeline is really a deathline. There is no parallel to paying taxes and living on the remainder. For it is not so much of our time and so much of our attention that God demands; it is not even all our time and all our attention: it is ourselves. For each of us the Baptist's words are true: 'He must increase and I decrease.' He will be infinitely merciful to our repeated failures; I know no promise that He will accept a deliberate compromise. For He has, in the last resort, nothing to give us but Himself; and He can give that only in so far as our self-affirming will retires and makes room for Him in our souls. Let us make up our minds to it; there will be nothing 'of our own' left over to live on; no 'ordinary' life. I do not mean that each of us will necessarily be called to be a martyr or even an ascetic. That's as may be. For some (nobody knows which) the Christian life will include much leisure, many occupations we naturally like. But these will be received from God's hands. In a perfect Christian they would be as much part of his 'religion', his 'service', as his hardest duties, and his feasts would be as Christian as his fasts. What cannot be admitted—what must exist only as an undefeated but daily resisted enemy—is the idea of something that is 'our own', some area in which we are to be 'out of school', on which God has no claim.

For he claims all, because He is love and must bless. He cannot bless us unless He has us. When we try to keep within us an area that is our own, we try to keep an area of death. Therefore, in love, He claims all. There's no bargaining with Him.

THE WEIGHT OF GLORY
"A Slip of the Tongue"

Between Right and Wrong

Scripture Readings
Romans 3:19–26
Psalm 106:6–15

Think of a country where people were admired for running away in battle, or where a man felt proud of double-crossing all the people who had been kindest to him.

You might just as well try to imagine a country where two and two made five. Men have differed as regards what people you ought to be unselfish to—whether it was only your own family, or your fellow countrymen, or everyone. But they have always agreed that you ought not to put yourself first. Selfishness has never been admired. Men have differed as to whether you should have one wife or four. But they have always agreed that you must not simply have any woman you liked.

But the most remarkable thing is this. Whenever you find a man who says he does not believe in a real Right and Wrong, you will find the same man going back on this a moment later. He may break his promise to you, but if you try breaking one to him he will be complaining 'It's not fair' before you can say Jack Robinson. A nation may say treaties don't matter; but then, next minute, they spoil their case by saying that the particular treaty they want to break was an unfair one. But if treaties do not matter, and if there is no such thing as Right and Wrong—in other words, if there is no Law of Nature—what is the difference between a fair treaty and an unfair one? Have they not let the cat out of the bag and shown that, whatever they say, they really know the Law of Nature just like anyone else?

It seems, then, we are forced to believe in a real Right and Wrong. People may be sometimes mistaken about them, just as people sometimes get their sums wrong; but they are not a matter of mere taste and opinion any more than the multiplication table. Now if we are agreed about that, I go on to my next point, which is this. None of us are really keeping the Law of Nature. If there are any exceptions among you, I apologise to them. They had much better read some other book, for nothing I am going to say concerns them. And now, turning to the ordinary human beings who are left:

I hope you will not misunderstand what I am going to say. I am not preaching, and Heaven knows I do not pretend to be better than anyone else. I am only trying to call attention to a fact; the fact that this year, or this month, or, more likely, this very day, we have failed to practise ourselves the kind of behaviour we expect from other people. There may be all sorts of excuses for us. That time you were so unfair to the children was when you were very tired. That slightly shady business about the money—the one you have almost forgotten—came when you were very hard-up. And what you promised to do for old So-and-so and have never done—well, you never would have promised if you had known how frightfully busy you were going to be. And as for your behaviour to your wife (or husband) or sister (or brother) if I knew how irritating they could be, I would not wonder at it—and who the dickens am I, anyway? I am just the same. That is to say, I do not succeed in keeping the Law of Nature very well, and the moment anyone tells me I am not keeping it, there starts up in my mind a string of excuses as long as your arm. The question at the moment is not whether they are good excuses. The point is that they are one more proof of how deeply, whether we like it or not, we believe in the Law of Nature. If we do not believe in decent behaviour, why should we be so anxious to make excuses for not having behaved decently? The truth is, we believe in decency so much—we feel the Rule of Law pressing on us so—that we cannot bear to face the fact that we are breaking it, and consequently we try to shift the responsibility. For you notice that it is only for our bad behaviour that we find all these explanations. It is only our bad temper that we put down to being tired or worried or hungry; we put our good temper down to ourselves.

These, then, are the two points I wanted to make. First, that human beings, all over the earth, have this curious idea that they ought to behave in a certain way, and cannot really get rid of it. Secondly, that they do not in fact behave in that way. They know the Law of Nature; they break it. These two facts are the foundation of all clear thinking about ourselves and the universe we live in.

MERE CHRISTIANITY
"The Law of Human Nature"

WEEK SEVEN

Exploring the Paradox of Suffering

Scripture Readings
Luke 19:26–46
Psalm 24:1–10

There is a paradox about tribulation in Christianity. Blessed are the poor, but by 'judgement' (i.e., social justice) and alms we are to remove poverty wherever possible. Blessed are we when persecuted, but we may avoid persecution by flying from city to city, and may pray to be spared it, as Our Lord prayed in Gethsemane. But if suffering is good, ought it not to be pursued rather than avoided? I answer that suffering is not good in itself. What is good in any painful experience is, for the sufferer, his submission to the will of God, and, for the spectators, the compassion aroused and the acts of mercy to which it leads. In the fallen and partially redeemed universe we may distinguish (1) the simple good descending from God, (2) the simple evil produced by rebellious creatures, and (3) the exploitation of that evil by God for His redemptive purpose, which produces (4) the complex good to which accepted suffering and repented sin contribute. Now the fact that God can make complex good out of simple evil does not excuse—though by mercy it may save—those who do the simple evil. And this distinction is central. Offences must come, but woe to those by whom they come; sins *do* cause grace to abound, but we must not make that an excuse for continuing to sin. The crucifixion itself is the best, as well as the worst, of all historical events, but the role of Judas remains simply evil. We may apply this first to the problem of other people's suffering. A merciful man aims at his neighbour's good and so does 'God's will', consciously co-operating with 'the simple good'. A cruel man oppresses his neighbour, and so does simple evil. But in doing such evil, he is used by God, without his own knowledge or consent, to produce the complex good—so that the first man serves God as a son, and the second as a tool. For you will certainly carry out God's purpose, however you act, but it makes a difference to you whether you serve like Judas or like John. The whole system is, so to speak, calculated for the clash between good men and bad men, and the good fruits of fortitude, patience, pity and forgiveness for which the cruel man is permitted to be cruel, presuppose that the good man ordinarily continues to seek simple good. I say 'ordinarily' because a man is sometimes entitled to hurt (or even, in my opinion, to kill) his fellow, but only where the necessity is urgent and the good to be attained obvious, and usually (though not always) when he who inflicts the pain has a definite authority to do so—a parent's authority derived from nature, a magistrate's or soldier's derived from civil society, or a surgeon's derived, most often, from the patient. To turn this into a general charter for afflicting humanity 'because affliction is good for them' (as Marlowe's lunatic Tamberlaine boasted himself the 'scourge of God') is not indeed to break the Divine scheme but to volunteer for the post of Satan within that scheme. If you do his work, you must be prepared for his wages.

The problem about avoiding our own pain admits a similar solution. Some ascetics have used self-torture. As a layman, I offer no opinion on the prudence of such a regimen; but I insist that, whatever its merits, self-torture is quite a different thing from tribulation sent by God. Everyone knows that fasting is a different experience from missing your dinner by accident or through poverty. Fasting asserts the will against the appetite—the reward being self-mastery and the danger pride: involuntary hunger subjects appetite and will together to the Divine will, furnishing an occasion for submission and exposing us to the danger of rebellion. But the redemptive effect of suffering lies chiefly in its tendency to reduce the rebel will. Ascetic practises, which in themselves strengthen the will, are only useful in so far as they enable the will to put its own house (the passions) in order, as a preparation for offering the whole man to God. They are necessary as a means; as an end, they would be abominable, for in substituting will for appetite and there stopping, they would merely exchange the animal self for the diabolical self. It was, therefore, truly said that 'only God can mortify'. Tribulation does its work in a world where human beings are ordinarily seeking, by lawful means, to avoid their own natural evil and to attain their natural good, and presupposes such a world. In order to submit the will to God, we must have a will and that will must have objects. Christian renunciation does not mean stoic 'Apathy', but a readiness to prefer God to inferior ends which are in themselves lawful. Hence the Perfect Man brought to Gethsemane a will, and a strong will, to escape suffering and death if such escape were compatible with the Father's will, combined with a perfect readiness for obedience if it were not. Some of the saints recommend a 'total renunciation' at the very threshold of our discipleship; but I think this can mean only a total readiness for every particular renunciation that may be demanded, for it would not be possible to live from moment to moment willing nothing but submission to God as such. What would be the *material* for the submission? It would seem self-contradictory to say 'What I will is to subject what I will to God's will,' for the second *what* has no content. Doubtless we all spend too much care in the avoidance of our own pain: but a duly subordinated intention to avoid it, using lawful means, is in accordance with 'nature'—that is, with the whole working system of creaturely life for which the redemptive work of tribulation is calculated.

It would be quite false, therefore, to suppose that the Christian view of suffering is incompatible with the strongest emphasis on our duty to leave the world, even in a temporal sense, 'better' than we found it. In the fullest parabolic picture which He gave of the Judgement, Our Lord seems to reduce all virtue to active beneficence: and though it would be misleading to take that one picture in isolation from the Gospel as a whole, it is sufficient to place beyond doubt the basic principles of the social ethics of Christianity.

THE PROBLEM OF PAIN
"Human Pain, Continued"

The Appetite for God

Scripture Readings
Luke 19:45–48
Psalm 25:8–22

When the Psalmists speak of 'seeing' the Lord, or long to 'see' Him, most of them mean something that happened to them in the Temple. The fatal way of putting this would be to say, 'They only mean they have seen the festival.' It would be better to say, 'If we had been there we should have seen only the festival.' Thus in Psalm 68 'It is well seen, O God, how thou goest . . . in the sanctuary . . . the singers go before, the minstrels follow after; in the midst are the damsels playing with the timbrels' (24, 25), it is almost as if the poet said, 'Look, here He comes.' If I had been there I should have seen the musicians and the girls with the tambourines; in addition, as another thing, I might or might not have (as we say) 'felt' the presence of God. The ancient worshipper would have been aware of no such dualism. Similarly, if a modern man wished to 'dwell in the house of the Lord all the days of his life, to behold the fair beauty of the Lord' (Ps. 27:4) he would mean, I suppose, that he hoped to receive, not of course without the mediation of the sacraments and the help of other 'services', but as something distinguishable from them and not to be presumed upon as their inevitable result, frequent moments of spiritual vision and the 'sensible' love of God. But I suspect that the poet of that Psalm drew no distinction between 'beholding the fair beauty of the Lord' and the acts of worship themselves.

When the mind becomes more capable of abstraction and analysis this old unity breaks up. And no sooner is it possible to distinguish the rite from the vision of God than there is a danger of the rite becoming a substitute for, and a rival to, God Himself. Once it can be thought of separately, it will; and it may then take on a rebellious, cancerous life of its own. There is a stage in a child's life at which it cannot separate the religious from the merely festal character of Christmas or Easter. I have been told of a very small and very devout boy who was heard murmuring to himself on Easter morning a poem of his own composition which began 'Chocolate eggs and Jesus risen'. This seems to me, for his age, both admirable poetry and admirable piety. But of course the time will soon come when such a child can no longer effortlessly and spontaneously enjoy that unity. He will become able to distinguish the spiritual from the ritual and festal aspect of Easter; chocolate eggs will no longer be sacramental. And once he has distinguished he must put one or the other first. If he puts the spiritual first he can still taste something of Easter in the chocolate eggs; if he puts the eggs first they will soon be no more than any other sweetmeat. They have taken on an independent, and therefore a soon withering, life. Either at some period in Judaism, or else in the experience of some Jews, a roughly parallel situation occurred. The unity falls apart; the sacrificial rites become distinguishable from the meeting with God. This does not unfortunately mean that they will cease or become less important. They may, in various evil modes, become even more important than before. They may be valued as a sort of commercial transaction with a greedy God who somehow really wants or needs large quantities of carcasses and whose favours cannot be secured on any other terms. Worse still, they may be regarded as the only thing He wants, so that their punctual performance will satisfy Him without obedience to His demands for mercy, 'judgement', and truth. To the priests themselves the whole system will seem important simply because it is both their art and their livelihood; all their pedantry, all their pride, all their economic position, is bound up with it. They will elaborate their art more and more. And of course the corrective to these views of sacrifice can be found within Judaism itself. The prophets continually fulminate against it. Even the Psalter, though largely a Temple collection, can do so; as in Psalm 50 where God tells His people that all this Temple worship, considered in itself, is not the real point at all, and particularly ridicules the genuinely Pagan notion that He really needs to be fed with roast meat. 'If I were hungry, do you think I would apply to *you*?' (12). I have sometimes fancied He might similarly ask a certain type of modern clergyman, 'If I wanted music—if I were conducting research into the more recondite details of the history of the Western Rite—do you really think you are the source I would rely on?'

This possible degradation of sacrifice and the rebukes of it are, however, so well known that there is no need to stress them here. I want to stress what I think that we (or at least I) need more; the joy and delight in God which meet us in the Psalms, however loosely or closely, in this or that instance, they may be connected with the Temple. This is the living centre of Judaism. These poets knew far less reason than we for loving God. They did not know that He offered them eternal joy; still less that He would die to win it for them. Yet they express a longing for Him, for His mere presence, which comes only to the best Christians or to Christians in their best moments. They long to live all their days in the Temple so that they may constantly see 'the fair beauty of the Lord' (Ps. 27:4). Their longing to go up to Jerusalem and 'appear before the presence of God' is like a physical thirst (Ps. 42). From Jerusalem His presence flashes out 'in perfect beauty' (Ps. 50:2). Lacking that encounter with Him, their souls are parched like a waterless countryside

(Ps. 63:2). They crave to be 'satisfied with the pleasures' of His house (Ps. 65:4). Only there can they be at ease, like a bird in the nest (Ps. 84:3). One day of those 'pleasures' is better than a lifetime spent elsewhere (Ps. 84:10).

I have rather—though the expression may seem harsh to some—called this the 'appetite for God' than 'the love of God'. The 'love of God' too easily suggests the word 'spiritual' in all those negative or restrictive senses which it has unhappily acquired. These old poets do not seem to think that they are meritorious or pious for having such feelings; nor, on the other hand, that they are privileged in being given the grace to have them. They are at once less priggish about it than the worst of us and less humble—one might almost say, less surprised—than the best of us. It has all the cheerful spontaneity of a natural, even a physical, desire. It is gay and jocund. They are glad and rejoice (Ps. 9:2). Their fingers itch for the harp (Ps. 43:4), for the lute and the harp—wake up, lute and harp!—(Ps. 57:9); let's have a song, bring the tambourine, bring the 'merry harp with the lute', we're going to sing merrily and make a cheerful noise (Ps. 81:1, 2). Noise, you may well say. Mere music is not enough. Let everyone, even the benighted gentiles, clap their hands (Ps. 47:1). Let us have clashing cymbals, not only well tuned, but *loud*, and dances too (Ps. 150:5). Let even the remote islands (all islands were remote, for the Jews were no sailors) share the exultation (Ps. 97:1).

I am not saying that this gusto—if you like, this

rowdiness—can or should be revived. Some of it cannot be revived because it is not dead but with us still. It would be idle to pretend that we Anglicans are a striking example. The Romans, the Orthodox, and the Salvation Army all, I think, have retained more of it than we. We have a terrible concern about good taste. Yet even we can still exult. The second reason goes far deeper. All Christians know something the Jews did not know about what it 'cost to redeem their souls'. Our life as Christians begins by being baptised into a death; our most joyous festivals begin with, and centre upon, the broken body and the shed blood. There is thus a tragic depth in our worship which Judaism lacked. Our joy has to be the sort of joy which can coexist with that; there is for us a spiritual counterpoint where they had simple melody. But this does not in the least cancel the delighted debt which I, for one, feel that I owe to the most jocund Psalms. There, despite the presence of elements we should now find it hard to regard as religious at all, and the absence of elements which some might think essential to religion, I find an experience fully God-centred, asking of God no gift more urgently than His presence, the gift of Himself, joyous to the highest degree, and unmistakably real. What I see (so to speak) in the faces of these old poets tells me more about the God whom they and we adore.

REFLECTIONS ON THE PSALMS
"The Fair Beauty of the Lord"

The Lesson of the Fig Tree

Scripture Readings
Matthew 21:16–22
Psalm 105:23–45

Christ's single miracle of Destruction, the withering of the fig-tree, has proved troublesome to some people, but I think its significance is plain enough. The miracle is an acted parable, a symbol of God's sentence on all that is 'fruitless' and specially, no doubt, on the official Judaism of that age. That is its moral significance. As a miracle, it again does in focus, repeats small and close, what God does constantly and throughout Nature. We have seen . . . how God, twisting Satan's weapon out of his hand, had become, since the Fall, the God even of human death. But much more, and perhaps ever since the creation, He has been the God of the death of organisms. In both cases, though in somewhat different ways, He is the God of death because He is the God of Life: the God of human death because through it increase of life now comes—the God of merely organic death because death is part of the very mode by which organic life spreads itself out in Time and yet remains new. A forest a thousand years deep is still collectively alive because some trees are dying and others are growing up. His human face, turned with negation in its eyes upon that one fig-tree, did once what His unincarnate action does to all trees. No tree died that year in Palestine, or any year anywhere, except because God did—or rather ceased to do—something to it.

All the miracles which we have considered so far are Miracles of the Old Creation. In all of them we see the Divine Man focusing for us what the God of Nature has already done on a larger scale. In our next class, the Miracles of Dominion over the Inorganic, we find some that are of the Old Creation and some that are of the New. When Christ stills the storm He does what God has often done before. God made Nature such that there would be both storms and calms: in that way all storms (except those that are still going on at this moment) have been stilled by God. It is unphilosophical, if you have once accepted the Grand Miracle, to reject the stilling of the storm. There is really no difficulty about adapting the weather conditions of the rest of the world to this one miraculous calm. I myself can still a storm in a room by shutting the window. Nature must make the best she can of it. And to do her justice she makes no trouble at all. The whole system, far from being thrown out of gear (which is what some nervous people seem to think a miracle would do) digests the new situation as easily as an elephant digests a drop of water. She is, as I have said before, an accomplished hostess. But when Christ walks on the water we have a miracle of the New Creation. God had not made the Old Nature, the world before the Incarnation, of such a kind that water would support a human body. This miracle is the foretaste of a Nature that is still in the future. The New creation is just breaking in. For a moment it looks as if it were going to spread. For a moment two men are living in that new world. St Peter also walks on the water—a pace or two: then his trust fails him and he sinks. He is back in Old Nature. That momentary glimpse was a snowdrop of a miracle. The snowdrops show that we have turned the corner of the year. Summer is coming. But it is a long way off and the snowdrops do not last long.

MIRACLES
"Miracles of the Old Creation"

The Appeal of Christianity According to Screwtape

Scripture Readings
Luke 22:1–8
Psalm 141:1–10

The Screwtape Letters is a correspondence from a senior demon to his apprentice. Because today is the traditional day to recognize Judas's deceit, an excerpt from a devil's point of view seems appropriate.

My dear Wormwood,

Through this girl and her disgusting family the patient is now getting to know more Christians every day, and very intelligent Christians too. For a long time it will be quite impossible to *remove* spirituality from his life. Very well then; we must *corrupt* it. No doubt you have often practised transforming yourself into an angel of light as a parade-ground exercise. Now is the time to do it in the face of the Enemy. The World and the Flesh have failed us; a third Power remains. And success of this third kind is the most glorious of all. A spoiled saint, a Pharisee, an inquisitor, or a magician, makes better sport in Hell than a mere common tyrant or debauchee.

Looking round your patient's new friends I find that the best point of attack would be the borderline between theology and politics. Several of his new friends are very much alive to the social implications of their religion. That, in itself, is a bad thing; but good can be made out of it.

You will find that a good many Christian-political writers think that Christianity began going wrong, and departing from the doctrine of its Founder, at a very early stage. Now this idea must be used by us to encourage once again the conception of a 'historical Jesus' to be found by clearing away later 'accretions and perversions' and then to be contrasted with the whole Christian tradition. In the last generation we promoted the construction of such a 'historical Jesus' on liberal and humanitarian lines; we are now putting forward a new 'historical Jesus' on Marxian, catastrophic, and revolutionary lines. The advantages of these constructions, which we intend to change every thirty years or so, are manifold. In the first place they all tend to direct men's devotion to something which does not exist, for each 'historical Jesus' is unhistorical. The documents say what they say and cannot be added to; each new 'historical Jesus' therefore has to be got out of them by suppression at one point and exaggeration at another, and by that sort of guessing (*brilliant* is the adjective we teach humans to apply to it) on which no one would risk ten shillings in ordinary life, but which is enough to produce a crop of new Napoleons, new Shakespeares, and new Swifts, in every publisher's autumn list. In the second place, all such constructions place the importance of their historical Jesus in some peculiar theory He is supposed to have promulgated. He has to be a 'great man' in the modern sense of the word—one standing at the terminus of some centrifugal and unbalanced line of thought—a crank vending a panacea. We thus distract men's minds from who He is, and what He did. We first make Him solely a teacher, and then conceal the very substantial agreement between His teachings and those of all other great moral teachers. For humans must not be allowed to notice that all great moralists are sent by the Enemy not to inform men but to remind them, to restate the primeval moral platitudes against our continual concealment of them. We make the Sophists: He raises up a Socrates to answer them. Our third aim is, by these constructions, to destroy the devotional life. For the real presence of the Enemy, otherwise experienced by men in prayer and sacrament, we substitute a merely probable, remote, shadowy, and uncouth figure, one who spoke a strange language and died a long time ago. Such an object cannot in fact be worshipped. Instead of the Creator adored by its creature, you soon have merely a leader acclaimed by a partisan, and finally a distinguished character approved by a judicious historian. And fourthly, besides being unhistorical in the Jesus it depicts, religion of this kind is false to history in another sense. No nation, and few individuals, are really brought into the Enemy's camp by the historical study of the biography of Jesus, simply as biography. Indeed materials for a full biography have been withheld from men. The earliest converts were converted by a single historical fact (the Resurrection) and a single theological doctrine (the Redemption) operating on a sense of sin which they already had—and sin, not against some new fancy-dress law produced as a novelty by a 'great man', but against the old, platitudinous, universal moral law which they had been taught by their nurses and mothers. The 'Gospels' come later and were written not to make Christians but to edify Christians already made.

The 'historical Jesus' then, however dangerous He may seem to be to us at some particular point, is always to be encouraged. About the general connection between Christianity and politics, our position is more delicate. Certainly we do not want men to allow their Christianity to flow over into their political life, for the establishment of anything like a really just society would be a major disaster. On the other hand we do want, and want very much, to make men treat Christianity as a means; preferably, of course, as a means to their own advancement, but, failing that, as a means to anything—even to social justice. The thing to do is to get a man at first to value social justice as a thing which the Enemy demands, and then work him on to the stage at which he values Christianity because it may produce social justice. For the Enemy will not be used as a convenience. Men or nations who think they can revive the Faith in order to make a good society might just as well think they can use the stairs of Heaven as a short cut to the nearest chemist's shop. Fortunately it is quite easy to coax humans round this little corner. Only today I have found a passage in a Christian writer where he recommends his own version of Christianity on the ground that 'only such a faith can outlast the death of old cultures and the birth of new civilisations'. You see the little rift? 'Believe this, not because it is true, but for some other reason.' That's the game,

Your affectionate uncle
SCREWTAPE

THE SCREWTAPE LETTERS
XXIII

The Power of Trust

Scripture Readings
John 13:1–11
Psalm 31:1–5

All may yet be well. This is true. Meanwhile you have the waiting—waiting till the X-rays are developed and till the specialist has completed his observations. And while you wait, you still have to go on living—if only one could go underground, hibernate, sleep it out. And then (for me—I believe you are stronger) the horrible by-products of anxiety; the incessant, circular movement of the thoughts, even the Pagan temptation to keep watch for irrational omens. And one prays; but mainly such prayers as are themselves a form of anguish.

Some people feel guilty about their anxieties and re-gard them as a defect of faith. I don't agree at all. They are afflictions, not sins. Like all afflictions, they are, if we can so take them, our share in the Passion of Christ. For the beginning of the Passion—the first move, so to speak—is in Gethsemane. In Gethsemane a very strange and significant thing seems to have happened.

It is clear from many of His sayings that Our Lord had long foreseen His death. He knew what conduct such as His, in a world such as we have made of this, must inevitably lead to. But it is clear that this knowledge must somehow have been withdrawn from Him before He prayed in Gethsemane. He could not, with whatever reservation about the Father's will, have prayed that the cup might pass and simultaneously known that it would not. That is both a logical and a psychological impossibility. You see what this involves? Lest any trial incident to humanity should be lacking, the torments of hope—of suspense, anxiety—were at the last moment loosed upon Him—the supposed possibility that, after all, He might, He just conceivably might, be spared the supreme horror. There was precedent. Isaac had been spared: he too at the last moment, he also against all apparent probability. It was not quite impossible . . . and doubtless He had seen other men crucified . . . a sight very unlike most of our religious pictures and images.

But for this last (and erroneous) hope against hope, and the consequent tumult of the soul, the sweat of blood, perhaps He would not have been very Man. To live in a fully predictable world is not to be a man.

At the end, I know, we are told that an angel appeared 'comforting' him. But neither *comforting* in sixteenth-

195

century English nor ἐννισχύων in Greek means 'consoling'. 'Strengthening' is more the word. May not the strengthening have consisted in the renewed certainty—cold comfort this—that the thing must be endured and therefore could be?

We all try to accept with some sort of submission our afflictions when they actually arrive. But the prayer in Gethsemane shows that the preceding anxiety is equally God's will and equally part of our human destiny. The perfect Man experienced it. And the servant is not greater than the master. We are Christians, not Stoics.

Does not every movement in the Passion write large some common element in the sufferings of our race? First, the prayer of anguish; not granted. Then He turns to His friends. They are asleep—as ours, or we, are so often, or busy, or away, or preoccupied. Then He faces the Church; the very Church that He brought into existence. It condemns Him. This is also characteristic. In every Church, in every institution, there is something which sooner or later works against the very purpose for which it came into existence. But there seems to be another chance. There is the State; in this case, the Roman state. Its pretensions are far lower than those of the Jewish church, but for that very reason it may be free from local fanaticisms. It claims to be just, on a rough, worldly level. Yes, but only so far as is consistent with political expediency and *raison d'état*. One becomes a counter in a complicated game. But even now all is not lost. There is still an appeal to the People—the poor and simple whom He had blessed, whom He had healed and fed and taught, to whom He himself belongs. But they have become over-night (it is nothing unusual) a murderous rabble shouting for His blood. There is, then, nothing left but God. And to God, God's last words are, 'Why hast thou forsaken me?'

You see how characteristic, how representative, it all is. The human situation writ large. These are among the things it means to be a man. Every rope breaks when you seize it. Every door is slammed shut as you reach it. To be like the fox at the end of the run; the earths all staked.

As for the last dereliction of all, how can we either understand or endure it? Is it that God Himself cannot be Man unless God seems to vanish at His greatest need? And if so, why? I sometimes wonder if we have even begun to understand what is involved in the very concept of creation. If God will create, He will make something to be, and yet to be not Himself. To be created is, in some sense, to be ejected or separated. Can it be that the more perfect the creature is, the further this separation must at some point be pushed? It is saints, not common people, who experience the 'dark night'. It is men and angels, not beasts, who rebel. Inanimate matter sleeps in the bosom of the Father. The 'hiddenness' of God perhaps presses most painfully on those who are in another way nearest to Him, and therefore God Himself, made man, will of all men be by God most forsaken? One of the seventeenth-century divines says: 'By pretending to be visible God could only deceive the world.' Perhaps He does pretend just a little to simple souls who need a full measure of 'sensible consolation'. Not deceiving them, but tempering the wind to the shorn lamb. Of course I'm not saying like Niebühr that evil is inherent in finitude. That would identify the creation with the fall and make God the author of evil. But perhaps there is an anguish, an alienation, a crucifixion involved in the creative act. Yet He who alone can judge judges the far-off consummation to be worth it.

LETTERS TO MALCOLM, CHIEFLY ON PRAYER
Chapter 8

Making Sense of the Story of Christ

Scripture Readings
Matthew 27:1–54
Psalm 22:1–11

Now, as a literary historian, I am perfectly convinced that whatever else the Gospels are they are not legends. I have read a great deal of legend and I am quite clear that they are not the same sort of thing. They are not artistic enough to be legends. From an imaginative point of view they are clumsy, they don't work up to things properly. Most of the life of Jesus is totally unknown to us, as is the life of anyone else who lived at that time, and no people building up a legend would allow that to be so. Apart from bits of the Platonic dialogues, there are no conversations that I know of in ancient literature like the Fourth Gospel. There is nothing, even in modern literature, until about a hundred years ago when the realistic novel came into existence. In the story of the woman taken in adultery we are told Christ bent down and scribbled in the dust with His finger. Nothing comes of this. No one has ever based any doctrine on it. And the art of *inventing* little irrelevant details to make an imaginary scene more convincing is a purely modern art. Surely the only explanation of this passage is that the thing really happened? The author put it in simply because he had *seen* it.

Then we come to the strangest story of all, the story of the Resurrection. It is very necessary to get the story clear. I heard a man say, 'The importance of the Resurrection is that is gives evidence of survival, evidence that the human personality survives death.' On that view what happened to Christ would be what had always happened to all men, the difference being that in Christ's case we were privileged to see it happening. This is certainly not what the earliest Christian writers thought. Something perfectly new in the history of the universe had happened. Christ had defeated death. The door, which had always been locked, had for the very first time been forced open. This is something quite distinct from mere ghost-survival. I don't mean that they disbelieved in ghost-survival. On the contrary, they believed in it so firmly that, on more than one occasion, Christ had had to assure them that He was *not* a ghost. The point is that while believing in survival they yet regarded the Resurrection as something totally different and new. The Resurrection narratives are not a picture of survival after death; they record how a totally new mode of being has arisen in the Universe. Something new had appeared in the Universe: as new as the first coming of organic life. This Man, after death, does not get divided into 'ghost' and 'corpse'. A new mode of being has arisen. That is the story. What are we going to make of it?

The question is, I suppose, whether any hypothesis covers the facts so well as the Christian hypothesis. That hypothesis is that God has come down into the created Universe, down to manhood—and come up again, pulling it up with Him. The alternative hypothesis is not legend, nor exaggeration, nor the apparitions of a ghost. It is either lunacy or lies. Unless one can take the second alternative (and I can't) one turns to the Christian theory.

'What are we to make of Christ?' There is no question of what we can make of Him; it is entirely a question of what He intends to make of us. You must accept or reject the story.

The things he says are very different from what any other teacher has said. Others say, 'This is the truth about the Universe. This is the way you ought to go,' but He says, 'I am the Truth, and the Way, and the Life.' He says, 'No man can reach absolute reality, except through Me. Try to retain your own life and you will be inevitably ruined. Give yourself away and you will be saved.' He says, 'If you are ashamed of Me, if, when you hear this call, you turn the other way, I also will look the other way when I come again as God without disguise. If anything whatever is keeping you from God and from me, whatever it is, throw it away. If it is your eye, pull it out. If it is your hand, cut it off. If you put yourself first you will be last. Come to Me everyone who is carrying a heavy load, I will set that right. Your sins, all of them, are wiped out, I can do that. I am Re-birth, I am Life. Eat Me, drink Me, I am your Food. And finally, do not be afraid, I have overcome the whole Universe.' That is the issue.

GOD IN THE DOCK
'What Are We to Make of Jesus Christ?'

The words from the Cross 'Why hast thou forsaken me' suggest that Our Lord entered into the human experience to the degree of complete dereliction and at one point no longer realised His own Deity nor foresaw His own Resurrection.

The gift was never withdrawn. Christ is still Man. Human nature has been taken up into the Divine Nature (see Athanasian Creed) and remains there. Our *bridgehead* is secure.

What do these people *want*? Do they actually visualise Him for 3 hours nailed to a stake—flayed back glued to unplaned wood—Palestinian sun—cloud of insects round head, hands, & feet—the face a mask of bruises, pus, spittle, blood, tears & sweat—the lungs gradually tearing owing to the position—and then complain 'This doesn't hurt enough?'

THE COLLECTED LETTERS OF C. S. LEWIS
Volume III, 9 May 1944

Visions of the Incarnation

Scripture Readings
Matthew 27:55–66
Psalm 2:1–12

The first reading is a letter to Audrey Sutherland. The second was written prior to Lewis's conversion but presents a vast, mysterious universe.

I believe you are right in thinking that most ancient peoples had no hope of heaven, tho' of course selected and exceptional individuals might be made gods and go to Olympus. That was as much out of the common course in their scheme as Elijah's being caught up in the fiery chariot is in ours. I won't answer for the Egyptians: nor for the Greek 'mystery' religions.

What is v. much more important is that the ancients may have been right. The N. T. always speaks of Christ not as one who taught, or demonstrated, the possibility of a glorious after life but as one who first created that possibility—the Pioneer, the First Fruits, the Man who forced the door. This of course links up with 1 Peter 3:20 about preaching to the spirits in prison and explains why Our Lord 'descended into Hell' (= *Sheol* or Hades). It looks v. much as if, till His resurrection, the fate of the dead actually *was* a shadowy half-life—mere ghosthood. The medieval authors delighted to picture what they called 'the harrowing of Hell', Christ descending and knocking on those eternal doors and bringing out those whom He chose. I believe in something like this. It wd. explain how what Christ did can save those who lived long before the Incarnation.

THE COLLECTED LETTERS OF C. S. LEWIS
Volume III, 28 April 1960

After the fret and failure of this day,
And weariness of thought, O Mother Night,
Come with soft kiss to soothe our care away
And all our little tumults set to right;
Most pitiful of all death's kindred fair,
Riding above us through the curtained air
On thy dusk car, thou scatterest to the earth
Sweet dreams and drowsy charms of tender might
And lovers' dear delight before tomorrow's birth.
Thus art thou wont thy quiet lands to leave

And pillared courts beyond the Milky Way,
Wherein thou tarriest all our solar day
While unsubstantial dreams before thee weave
A foamy dance, and fluttering fancies play
About thy palace in the silver ray
Of some far, moony globe. But when the hour,
The long-expected comes, the ivory gates
Open on noiseless hinge before thy bower
Unbidden, and the jewelled chariot waits
With magic steeds. Thou from the fronting rim
Bending to urge them, whilst thy sea-dark hair
Falls in ambrosial ripples o'er each limb,
With beautiful pale arms, untrammelled, bare
For horsemanship, to those twin chargers fleet
Dost give full rein across the fires that glow
In the wide floor of heaven, from off their feet
Scattering the powdery stardust as they go.
Come swiftly down the sky, O Lady Night,
Fall through the shadow-country, O most kind,
Shake out thy strands of gentle dreams and light
For chains, wherewith thou still art used to bind
With tenderest love of careful leeches' art
The bruised and weary heart
In slumber blind.

SPIRITS IN BONDAGE

"Night"

EASTER DAY

Rejoice in the Resurrection

Scripture Readings
Luke 24:1–53
Psalm 44:1–8

Out of our selves, into Christ, we must go. His will is to become ours and we are to think His thoughts, to 'have the mind of Christ' as the Bible says. And if Christ is one, and if He is thus to be 'in' us all, shall we not be exactly the same? It certainly sounds like it; but in fact it is not so.

It is difficult here to get a good illustration; because, of course, no other two things are related to each other just as the Creator is related to one of His creatures. But I will try two very imperfect illustrations which may give a hint of the truth. Imagine a lot of people who have always lived in the dark. You come and try to describe to them what light is like. You might tell them that if they come into the light that same light would fall on them all and they would all reflect it and thus become what we call visible. Is it not quite possible that they would imagine that, since they were all receiving the same light, and all reacting to it in the same way (i.e., all reflecting it), they would all look alike? Whereas you and I know that the light will in fact bring out, or show up, how different they are. Or again, suppose a person who knew nothing about salt. You give him a pinch to taste and he experiences a particular strong, sharp taste. You then tell him that in your country people use salt in all their cookery. Might he not reply, 'In that case I suppose all your dishes taste exactly the same: because the taste of that stuff you have just given me is so strong that it will kill the taste of everything else'? But you and I know that the real effect of salt is exactly the opposite. So far from killing the taste of the egg and the tripe and the cabbage, it actually brings it out. They do not show their real taste till you have added the salt. (Of course, as I warned you, this is not really a very good illustration, because you can, after all, kill the other tastes by putting in too much salt, whereas you cannot kill the taste of a human personality by putting in too much Christ. I am doing the best I can.)

It is something like that with Christ and us. The more we get what we now call 'ourselves' out of the way and let Him take us over, the more truly ourselves we become. There is so much of Him that millions and millions of 'little Christs', all different, will still be too few to express Him fully. He made them all. He invented—as an author invents characters in a novel—all the different men that you and I were intended to be. In that sense our real selves are all waiting for us in Him. It is no good trying to 'be myself' without Him. The more I resist Him and try to live on my own, the more I become dominated by my own heredity and upbringing and surroundings and natural desires. In fact what I so proudly call 'Myself' becomes merely the meeting place for trains of events which I never started and which I cannot stop. What I call 'My wishes' become merely the desires thrown up by my physical organism or pumped into me by other men's thoughts or even suggested to me by devils. Eggs and alcohol and a good night's sleep will be the real origins of what I flatter myself by regarding as my own highly personal and discriminating decision to make love to the girl opposite to me in the railway carriage. Propaganda will be the real origin of what I regard as my own personal political ideas. I am not, in my natural state, nearly so much of a person as I like to believe: most of what I call 'me' can be very easily explained. It is when I turn to Christ, when I give myself up to His Personality, that I first begin to have a real personality of my own.

At the beginning I said there were Personalities in God. I will go further now. There are no real personalities anywhere else. Until you have given up your self to Him you will not have a real self. Sameness is to be found most among the most 'natural' men, not among those who surrender to Christ. How monotonously alike all the great tyrants and conquerors have been: how gloriously different are the saints.

But there must be a real giving up of the self. You must throw it away 'blindly' so to speak. Christ will indeed give you a real personality: but you must not go to Him for the sake of that. As long as your own personality is what you are bothering about you are not going to Him at all. The very first step is to try to forget about the self altogether. Your real, new self (which is Christ's and also yours, and yours just because it is His) will not come as long as you are looking for it. It will come when you are looking for Him. Does that sound strange? The same principle holds, you know, for more everyday matters. Even in social life, you will never make a good impression on other people until you stop thinking about what sort of impression you are making. Even in literature and art, no man who bothers about originality will ever be original: whereas if you simply try to tell the truth (without caring twopence how often it has been told before) you will, nine times out of ten, become original without ever having noticed it. The principle runs through all life from top to bottom. Give up yourself, and you will find your real self. Lose your life and you will save it. Submit to death, death of your ambitions and favourite wishes every day and death of your whole body in the end: submit with every fibre of your being, and you will find eternal life. Keep back nothing. Nothing that you have not given away will be really yours. Nothing in you that has not died will ever be raised from the dead. Look for yourself, and you will find in the long run only hatred, loneliness, despair, rage, ruin, and decay. But look for Christ and you will find Him, and with Him everything else thrown in.

MERE CHRISTIANITY
"The New Men"

And as He spoke He no longer looked to them like a lion; but the things that began to happen after that were so great and beautiful that I cannot write them. And for us this is the end of all the stories, and we can most truly say that they all lived happily ever after. But for them it was only the beginning of the real story. All their life in this world and all their adventures in Narnia had only been the cover and the title page: now at last they were beginning Chapter One of the Great Story, which no one on earth has read: which goes on forever: in which every chapter is better than the one before.

THE LAST BATTLE
"Farewell to the Shadowlands"